Happy Cooking!

D1099111

SHOP LOCAL
EAT WELL

Kathryn Hawkins

NEW
HOLLAND

First published in 2008 by New Holland Publishers (UK) Ltd
London • Cape Town • Sydney • Auckland
www.newhollandpublishers.com

Garfield House
86–88 Edgware Road
London W2 2EA
United Kingdom

80 McKenzie Street, Cape Town, 8001, South Africa
Unit 1, 66 Gibbes Street, Chatswood, NSW 2067, Australia
218 Lake Road, Northcote, Auckland, New Zealand

ISBN 978 184537 992 6

Commissioning Editor: Clare Sayer
Production: Marion Storz
Design: Fiona Andreanelli (www.andreanelli.com)
Illustrations: Fiona Andreanelli & Vanessa Bowerman (www.foliotypo.com)
Editorial Direction: Rosemary Wilkinson

Reproduction by Modern Age Repro House, Hong Kong
Printed and bound in India by Replika Press Pvt. Ltd.

10 9 8 7 6 5 4 3 2 1

CONTENTS

Introduction 4

Spring 8
Summer 42
Autumn 76
Winter 110
Preserves & Accompaniments 144

Bibliography 174
Useful Addresses 174
Index 175
Acknowledgements 176

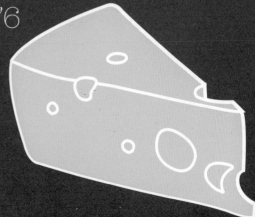

We are constantly being reminded of how to reduce our 'carbon footprint'; to cut down on waste, and to protect our environment before it's too late. This further reminder makes for a less than cheery opener to a cookery book! Yet, the type of food we buy and eat is one of the ways we can make significant changes to the world about us.

INTRODUCTION

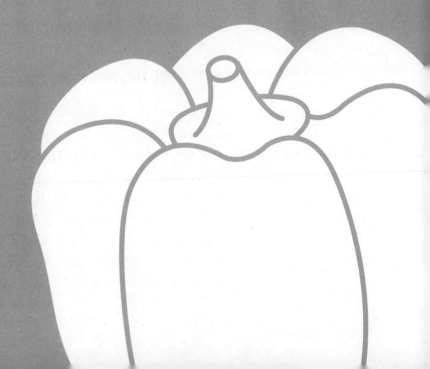

I'm not sure whether it has something to do with getting older and, hopefully, wiser, but since I quit the rat race, metropolitan life and a successful career, I've become seriously aware of my local environment and what it has to offer me. In London, I worked as a busy freelance food stylist, preparing food for photo shoots, and because I was constantly working three to six months ahead, I was always searching for foods out of season. Some things would cost an absolute fortune but they had to be found for a specific job – a few years ago, one April, I can remember paying £60 for a kilo of blackberries because they were flown in specially for me from Holland! Today, it is not that unusual to see strawberries on supermarket shelves in December, while other soft fruits and summer vegetables are flown in from far flung places of the globe like Chile, Morocco, Kenya and Thailand all year round.

Since moving to a more rural location, and breathing in fresher air, I've had the opportunity to buy locally grown produce and I am able to shop in independent shops where you're most likely to find produce from around the nearby vicinity. I'm also lucky enough now to have a big garden, and I can grow a few crops myself, which has made me more aware of the seasons. Once you start seeing what Mother Nature has to offer, it is quite easy to obey the seasons and you can really start to enjoy what's around naturally at specific times of the year. If we all changed our purchasing and eating habits, we'd be helping to reduce air miles in no time.

When fruit and vegetables are in season they look and taste so much better. A home-grown sweet, salmon-red, heart-shaped strawberry in June bears no resemblance to the deep red, tasteless monsters around at Christmas time. Admittedly, it is unlikely that we will ever be able to compete with the citrus groves of the Mediterranean or harvest the exotics from the Tropics here in the northern hemisphere, and to stop imports of such produce would be unreasonable, but we should try to choose more of our own produce and make the most of what we can grow and raise here.

Many of us have access to a butcher, baker, fishmonger and/or greengrocer, and farm shops and farmer's markets are increasingly popular; getting to know your local shopkeepers or farms will help you well on your way to finding out what's produced in your area. Even supermarkets are catching on to the notion that we want to eat more locally sourced goods, so look at the labels and see where the product has come from before putting it in your trolley. There are also many UK mail order companies that can send you all sorts of food through the post and it's worth checking out the web for information on produce that's seasonally available in another part of the country. You'll find more and more chefs choosing to use local produce on their menus, so you should support local businesses trying to do their bit too. It's getting easier day by day to enjoy local seasonal food.

I've divided my book into the four seasons of the year and highlighted what's good to eat at specific times. There are lots of hints and tips throughout which will hopefully inspire you into trying things that you might not have considered before. The final chapter contains a variety of recipes and tips for preserving fruits and vegetables to enable you to enjoy them out of season – one main advantage we have over our ancestors is the deep freeze: we can have juicy Summer berries in December that were grown just down the road! At the back of the book, you'll find some useful addresses and contacts to help you find out more about sourcing locally and how you can do more to help the environment around you. I hope you enjoy using this book as much as I have compiling it, and I wish you well in doing your bit to save the planet from your own doorstep!

My favourite season of the year. I think some of the nicest produce is around at this time: juicy Spring lamb, fine asparagus and the first of the Summer berries, the strawberry. There's also the anticipation of the warmer months ahead, with everything so fresh and green, it really is a special time.

SPRING

(beginning of March, through
April, to the end of May)

In March, we are still relying on a select few ingredients, and fruit is especially scarce, but the bright pink, tender stems of rhubarb still make a tempting choice. Once April arrives, we can say 'goodbye' to the starchy Winter roots and wholesome green vegetables, as the new tender crops like spinach are at their best. Look out for wild garlic and morel mushrooms when you're out and about in the woodlands and river ways at this time – free food is always a bonus, and these two are particularly tasty.

May is a special month for me; not only is it my birthday month, but I also think it is a particularly beautiful month for garden and wild flowers. The buds are fully burst open on the trees and many come into flower by the end of the month. The weather is often very good, and since moving to Perthshire, in Scotland, I have found May to be one of the best months of the year for getting out and about, and the air is still fresh but the warmth is creeping in. And, of course, my favourite foods come into season in May: asparagus and strawberries. You'll find some delicious recipes in this chapter which make the most of their subtle yet distinctive flavours, and the chocolate dipped strawberries that go with the Easter meringues on page 40 are a much-eaten personal favourite!

Apart from fruit and vegetables, lamb is the number one meat choice at this time of year and very succulent and full of flavour. The many cuts make it a versatile choice whatever the occasion. In the fishmongers, wild salmon is a luxurious treat to go with fresh asparagus, as is Dover or lemon sole. You'll see crab, most commonly the brown crab, but if you want something really special, ask your fishmonger to order you a spider crab – the flesh is sweeter, more flaky and more juicy. While you're investigating the fish counter, have a look out for samphire. This is a salty succulent plant that grows over sea shores. It needs thorough rinsing, but little other preparation or cooking, and adds a really salty 'bite' when served as an accompaniment to fish dishes.

Apples: Bramley	until May
Apples (dessert): Spartan/Cox's Orange/Pippin/Ida Red/ Laxton Superb/Crispin/Golden Delicious	until March
Asparagus	new season from mid March to July
Beans (hothouse)	new season from March to August
Broccoli	until April
Brussels sprouts	until March
Cabbage: Winter cabbages	until March
Cabbage: White	until April
Cabbage: Spring Greens	until April
Cabbage: Savoy	until May
Cabbage: Spring cabbage	until May
Celeriac	until March
Chicory	all year but at best until April
Endive	all year but at best until April
Elderflowers	harvest April to May
Gooseberries	new season from May to September
Horseradish	until March
Jerusalem Artichoke	until March
Kale	until May
Kohlrabi	until March
Leeks	until May
Marsh samphire	new season from April to July, but at best in May
Onions	until March
Parsnips	until April
Peaches (hothouse)	new season May to October
Pears (Conference)	until March
Peas	new season from May to October
Potatoes (maincrop)	until May
Potatoes (new)	new season from May to July
Radish	all year but at best in Spring
Rhubarb (forced)	until March
Salsify	until May
Sea Kale	until March
Shallots	until March
Spinach	all year but at best in Spring
Spring onion	all year but at best in Spring
Strawberries: cloche	new season from April to June
Strawberries: outdoors	new season from May to October
Swede	until May
Tomatoes	new season April to November
Turnips	until March
Wild garlic	harvest April until June
Wild mushrooms (morels)	harvest March/April

MEAT: lamb and duck
FISH: brill, cockles, crab, Dover sole, hake, halibut, John Dory, langoustines, lemon sole, mussels, plaice, oysters, sea bass, sea trout, wild salmon

Fresh cream of tomato and basil soup

A simple combination of ingredients that blend well together. It makes a perfectly light starter to any Spring meal, or a delicious light supper with some warm bread. Omit the cream for a fresher, healthier option.

Serves 4

1 quantity fresh tomato sauce (see page 157),
   replacing herbs with a few sprigs of fresh basil leaves
300 ml (10 fl oz) fresh vegetable stock (see page 156)
6 tbsp double cream
2 tsp caster sugar
Salt and freshly ground black pepper
A few fresh basil leaves to float

Make the tomato sauce as directed on page 157, using sprigs of fresh basil to flavour the tomatoes as they cook. Whilst hot, stir in the vegetable stock and 4 tbsp cream. Stir well and heat through until piping hot. Season with sugar and salt and pepper to taste.

Ladle into warmed serving bowls, and lightly swirl a little of the remaining cream into each portion. Sprinkle with a few basil leaves and grind over black pepper if liked. Serve immediately.

Note: For a chilled soup, allow the tomato sauce to cool and then mix in the stock and cream. Chill for at least and hour before serving over ice cubes.

Leek and wild garlic soup

In many shady areas or by water around Easter time, you'll smell the wafting aroma of wild garlic. Its bright green leaves are milder than the bulb type and perfect for more delicate flavours; I can't understand why it's such a neglected 'free' food.

Serves 4

50 g (2 oz) butter
450 g (1 lb) potatoes, peeled and diced
2 large leeks, trimmed, washed
    and white and green parts shredded
6 wild garlic leaves, well washed
1.2 l (40 fl oz) fresh chicken or vegetable stock (see page 156)
Salt and freshly ground black pepper
4 tbsp double cream

Melt the butter in a large saucepan until bubbling and then add the chopped potato, stir well in the butter, then cover and cook gently for about 10 minutes, stirring occasionally.

Meanwhile, finely shred 5 of the garlic leaves. Stir into the potatoes along with the leeks, and pour over half the stock. Bring to the boil, cover and simmer for about 30 minutes until tender. Cool for 10 minutes.

Transfer to a blender or food processor and blend until smooth. Return to the saucepan and add the remaining stock, seasoning and cream. Heat through until piping hot.

Ladle into warm serving bowls. Finely shred the remaining wild garlic and sprinkle a few shreds over each portion to serve.

Beef in red wine with green beans and morel mushrooms

Morel mushrooms are another Springtime 'freebie'. They can be found on light soil, near trees and hedgerows, and grow best on damp, warm days. They can be a bit fiddly to clean, but avoid soaking them as they will become spongy.

Serves 6

2 tbsp plain flour
Salt and freshly ground black pepper
900 g (2 lb) lean braising steak, trimmed and cut into 1 cm (½ in) thick pieces
2 tbsp vegetable oil
2 medium onions, peeled and chopped
2 garlic cloves, peeled and crushed
115 g (4 oz) rindless, unsmoked streaky bacon, chopped
300 ml (10 fl oz) dry red wine
300 ml (10 fl oz) fresh beef stock (see page 156)
2 bay leaves
225 g (8 oz) green beans
115 g (4 oz) morel mushrooms

Place the flour on a plate and season well. Toss the steak pieces in the seasoned flour until well coated. Heat the oil in a large pan or wok and gently fry the onion and garlic for 5 minutes until just softened. Add the steak with the flour and bacon and cook, stirring, for 5 minutes until the meat is browned and sealed all over.

Pour in the wine and stock and add the bay leaves. Bring to the boil, cover and simmer for 1½ hours. Remove the lid and cook for a further 15 minutes until tender.

Meanwhile, top and tail the beans and cut in to 5 cm (2 in) lengths. Bring a small saucepan of lightly salted water to the boil, cover and cook the beans for 3-4 minutes until just tender. Drain well and set aside. Trim away the base of the mushroom stalks. Slice larger mushrooms in half lengthways. Gently brush the mushrooms and then lightly wash and rinse to make sure they are completely free of earth. Shake well to remove excess water and gently pat dry using absorbent kitchen paper.

Stir the beans and mushrooms into the beef stew and cook for a further 5 minutes. Discard the bay leaves and adjust the seasoning before serving.

Moroccan-style spinach and chicken pie

Although available home grown all year round, spinach is usually at its best in the spring months. It has a slightly earthy flavour that goes very well with the warming spices cumin, coriander and cinnamon. Drain spinach well in order to help prevent the pastry becoming over-soft.

Serves 6

900 g (2 lb) fresh young spinach leaves, trimmed
115 g (4 oz) butter
1 tsp cumin seeds, lightly ground
1 tsp coriander seeds, lightly ground
1 large onion, peeled and finely chopped
50 g (2 oz) sultanas or chopped dried apricots
1 tsp ground cinnamon
Salt and freshly ground black pepper
6 large sheets filo pastry, thawed if frozen
300 g (10 oz) cooked free range chicken meat, diced

Rinse the spinach leaves and pack into a large saucepan whilst still wet. Cover and cook over a medium heat for 8–10 minutes, turning occasionally, until just wilted – the spinach will steam in the water that clings to the leaves. Drain well through a sieve or colander, pressing the spinach against the sides to extract as much water as possible. Leave aside, still draining, to cool.

Meanwhile, melt 25 g (1 oz) butter until bubbling and gently fry the spices with the onion over a gentle heat for 7–8 minutes, stirring occasionally, until softened but not browned. Stir in the sultanas and cinnamon and set aside to cool. Preheat the oven to 200°C (400°F, gas 6). Grease and line a 20 cm (8 in) round spring-form cake tin.

To assemble the pie, melt the remaining butter. Brush the prepared cake tin with melted butter and cover the base with a sheet of pastry, leaving the edges overhanging; brush with butter. Continue with the remaining sheets, brushing each with butter and leaving the edges overhanging. Arrange the chicken in the bottom of the tin.

Blot the cooled spinach with kitchen paper and then chop finely. Stir into the cooked onion mixture along with seasoning. Pile evenly on top of the chicken.

Fold the overhanging pastry over the spinach, piece by piece, brushing with butter as you go. Brush the top with any remaining butter and place the tin on a baking tray. Cook for 35–40 minutes until crisp and golden. Stand for 10 minutes before carefully releasing from the tin to serve. Best served hot or warm.

Spring lamb noisettes with mint and caramelised salsify

Juicy sweet lamb is at its best at this time of year, and is delicious married with a root vegetable. Salsify is an under-used root, but this is a delicious way to try it, and its natural slight earthy and globe artichoke-like flavour goes very well with roast meats.

Serves 4

1 quantity of mint sauce (see page 152)
4 x 115 g (4 oz) lamb noisettes
Salt and freshly ground black pepper
Juice of 1 lemon
675 g (1½ lb) salsify
Salt and freshly ground black pepper
75 g (3 oz) butter
1 tbsp light brown sugar
1 tbsp sunflower oil
Freshly chopped mint to garnish

Make up the mint sauce as described on page 152. Discard the packing string from the niosettes, then wash and pat dry with kitchen paper. Re-tie with clean string and season on both sides. Place in a shallow non-reactive dish and spoon 1 Tbsp mint sauce over each. Set aside whilst cooking the salsify.

Put the lemon juice in a large bowl and half fill with water. Peel the salsify and keep in the lemony water to prevent discolouring. Cut into slices of equal thickness, about 5-cm (2-in) lengths. Drain and place in a saucepan with a pinch of salt and cover with water. Bring to the boil and cook for 6–7 minutes until slightly tender. Drain well. Melt 50 g (2 oz) butter in a frying pan and stir in the sugar until it dissolves. Add the salsify, tossing well in the buttery syrup, and cook over a medium heat, stirring occasionally, for about 10 minutes until tender and lightly golden. Drain well and keep warm.

Drain the lamb. Heat the remaining butter with the oil in a frying pan until melted and bubbling. Cook the noisettes for 5–6 minutes on each side, or until cooked to your liking.

Pile the salsify on to warm serving plates and top each with a lamb noisette. Sprinkle with chopped mint and serve with green vegetables and the remaining mint sauce as an accompaniment.

Easter 'Guard of Honour' with leek and rosemary stuffing

This cut of meat makes an extra special roast lunch, perfect for serving over Easter when lamb is new season. Serve with either classic mint sauce (see page 152), or some home made redcurrant jelly (see page 153).

Serves 6

2 best-end of neck of lamb, each with 8 cutlets, chined
25 g (1 oz) butter
1 tbsp cold pressed rapeseed oil
1 large leek, trimmed and finely shredded
2 tbsp freshly chopped rosemary
75 g (3 oz) fresh white breadcrumbs
Salt and freshly ground black pepper
1 medium free range egg yolk
2 tbsp heather honey or other well flavoured locally produced honey

Using a sharp knife, trim the skin and fat from in between and around the bones at one end of the lamb cutlets. Scrape and clean the bones, leaving about 4 cm (1½ in) bone exposed. Slice off the brown rind to expose the creamy white fat underneath. Score the fat in a criss-cross pattern. Cover the exposed bones with foil. Set aside.

Heat the butter with the oil in a frying pan until bubbling and gently fry the leek, stirring, for 3–4 minutes until just softened. Place the remaining ingredients, except the honey, in a bowl and mix in the cooked leeks. Stir to form a firm stuffing mixture and set aside. Preheat the oven to 180°C (350°F, gas 4).

Line a chopping board with baking parchment. Place the lamb cutlets on the board, then position the cutlets facing each other so that the bone tips cross and interlace. Press the stuffing into the central cavity between the two lamb joints. Using the baking parchment, lift the stuffed lamb and weigh. Calculate the cooking time at 25 minutes per 450 g (1 lb) plus 25 minutes.

Transfer the lamb to a roasting tin and discard the parchment. Using a length of clean string, secure cutlets at both ends of the joint. In a small saucepan, gently soften the honey and brush over the lamb. Cook the lamb in the oven for the calculated cooking time, covering completely with foil after 1 hour, until the lamb is tender and cooked through to your liking.

To serve, discard the foil and string and place on a warmed serving dish. Ideal accompanied with new potatoes and freshly cooked green vegetables.

Ham shank with peas and parsley sauce

Peas go well with a very savoury meat like ham. There's very little preparation involved in this dish, yet it tastes great. Serve simply with creamy mashed potato. Any leftover ham cooking water makes a great base for soups and sauces.

Serves 4

2 x 1 kg (2 lb 3½ oz) smoked ham shanks
50 g (2 oz) parsley with stems
2 bay leaves
1 carrot, peeled
1 stick celery, trimmed
1 onion, peeled
2 tsp black peppercorns, lightly crushed
900 g (2 lb) fresh peas, shelled
3 tbsp cornflour
300 ml (10 fl oz) whole milk
¼ tsp ground nutmeg
Salt to taste

Trim away the rind from shanks, then put in a large saucepan and just cover with water. Cut the stalks from the parsley and add to the pan along with the bay leaves, carrot, celery, onion and peppercorns. Bring to the boil, cover and simmer for 1½ hours until tender and falling off the bone.

Carefully drain the shanks, retaining the cooking liquid, and strip away the meat into bite-sized chunks, discarding the fat and bone, and place in a heatproof dish. Spoon a little of the cooking water over the meat and keep warm.

Transfer sufficient ham cooking water to a saucepan for cooking the peas. Bring to the boil and add the peas. Cook for 5–6 minutes until just tender, drain and keep warm. Chop the parsley leaves finely and set aside.

In another saucepan, blend the cornflour with a little of the milk until smooth and paste-like. Stir in the remaining milk and 300 ml (10 fl oz) of the ham cooking liquid. Heat stirring, until boiling, and cook for 1 minute to thicken. Stir in the chopped parsley and ground nutmeg. Taste and season if necessary.

Serve pieces of ham on a bed of cooked peas and pour over sauce. Accompany with mashed potato.

Herby egg rolls of chicken, cucumber and pea shoots

These fresh tasting, crunchy wraps are good for a 'healthy' portable lunch – they are easy to pack and won't get soggy! You can add other ingredients of your choice as fillings such as cooked asparagus, raw spinach, baby salad leaves or sprouting seeds.

Serves 2

4 large free range eggs
Finely grated rind 1 small lemon
2 tbsp water
4 tbsp freshly chopped basil
Salt and freshly ground black pepper
2 tsp cold pressed rapeseed oil
4 tbsp mayonnaise (see page 154)
15-cm (6-in) piece cucumber, washed and cut into thin lengthways strips
A handful of fresh pea shoots
175g (6 oz) cooked free range chicken meat, cut into thin strips

Beat the eggs in a jug with the lemon rind, water, chopped basil and seasoning until well combined. Brush an 15cm (6 in) (base diameter) non stick frying pan with a little of the oil and place over a medium heat until hot. Pour in one quarter of the egg mixture, and cook for about a minute until set, tilting the pan to make sure the egg cooks evenly.

Slide a spatula under the egg and turn over. Cook for a further minute until just cooked. Transfer to a wire rack lined with baking parchment to cool. Repeat with the remaining egg mixture, brushing the pan with oil as necessary, to make four omelettes in total. When cool, stack between layers of baking parchment on a plate, cover and chill until required.

To assemble, spread each omelette with 1 tbsp mayonnaise and arrange cucumber strips, pea shoots and chicken down the centre of each. Roll up tightly, cover and chill until ready to serve. Best cut into two halves for easy eating.

Slow roast pork belly with apple mash

Belly pork needs long slow cooking to be enjoyed at its best. Here it is slow-cooked on a bed of apples and onions with a hint of sage, all of which get added to mashed potato to serve. You'll need to start the pork preparation the day before in order to get the best crackling ever!

Serves 4

1 kg (2 lb 3½ oz) piece pork belly, boned, with rind left on
1 tbsp sunflower oil
1 tbsp coarse salt, lightly crushed
2 medium onions, peeled and sliced
450 g (1 lb) cooking apples, cored, peeled and chopped
Juice of 1 lemon
40 g (1½ oz) light brown sugar
A few sprigs fresh sage
Salt and freshly ground black pepper
900 g (2 lb) floury potatoes, for mashing, peeled and diced

Wash and pat dry the pork thoroughly. Place in a large shallow dish and leave uncovered in the fridge overnight.

The next day, preheat the oven to 240°C (475°F, gas 9). Transfer the pork to a shallow roasting tin and brush lightly with oil. Sprinkle evenly with the crushed salt and bake for 20 minutes. Remove from the oven and reduce the heat to 170°C (325°F, gas 3).

In another roasting tin, mix the onions with the apples, lemon juice and sugar. Break up the sage, push into the mix and season generously with black pepper. Drain the pork and sit it on top. Cook for about 3 hours, checking occasionally to ensure the onions and apples aren't drying out – add a few tablespoons of water if they are.

Towards the end of cooking time, put the potatoes in a saucepan with a pinch of salt. Cover with water, bring to the boil and cook for 12–15 minutes until tender. Drain well and return to the saucepan. Mash well and keep warm.

Once the pork is cooked, place on a warm plate and keep warm. Discard the sage leaves from the onion and apple mixture. Using a slotted spoon, drain the onion and apple mixture into the mashed potatoes and mix well, adding some of the remaining cooking juices if liked. Taste and season if necessary.

To serve, remove the pork crackling and break into pieces. Cut the belly meat into chunky pieces. Divide the mash between warm shallow serving bowls and top with pork belly and cracking. Serve with green vegetables.

Pasta with roast salmon and asparagus

The first season's asparagus is due in May, and this heralds the start of my favourite time of year. Asparagus is my number one vegetable, and nothing can beat it if it's freshly harvested. Apart from steaming and serving with melted butter, roasting is an excellent way to serve it.

Serves 4

350 g (12 oz) fresh fine asparagus
   spears
2 tbsp cold pressed rapeseed oil
Salt and freshly ground black pepper
4 x 175-g (6-oz) salmon fillets
2 tsp dill or caraway seeds, lightly
   crushed
450 g (1 lb) fresh penne pasta
25 g (1 oz) butter
Juice and finely grated rind 1 small
   lemon
A few sprigs fresh dill, lightly chopped

Preheat the oven to 200°C (400°F, gas 6). Trim about 2.5 cm (1 in) away from the woody ends of the asparagus and arrange flat on a baking sheet. Brush with 1 tbsp oil and bake in the oven for about 25 minutes, turning occasionally, until tender and lightly crisp.

Wash and pat dry the salmon. Season all over, and place on top of the asparagus after about 5 minutes cooking time. Drizzle lightly with the remaining oil and sprinkle with the seeds. Bake in the oven for about 20 minutes, depending on thickness, until just cooked through. Drain and keep warm.

Bring a large saucepan of lightly salted water to the boil and cook the pasta according to the manufacturer's instructions. Drain well and return to the saucepan. Add the butter and lemon juice and rind and stir until melted and the pasta is well coated. Keep warm.

Cut the asparagus into short lengths, and lightly flake the salmon, discarding the skin. Carefully toss into the cooked pasta along with the dill. Serve immediately, piled into warmed pasta bowls.

Cockle and clam chowder

This rich seafood concoction makes a fabulous main meal with some crusty bread to mop up the sauce and a crisp salad to add texture. Cooked this way, the seafood is sweet and tender. Replace the clams with mussels if preferred.

Serves 4

1 tbsp cold pressed rapeseed oil
675 g (1½ lb) cockles, scrubbed and well rinsed
675 g (1½ lb) small clams, cleaned thoroughly
150 ml (5fl oz) dry white wine
25 g (1 oz) butter
2 shallots, peeled and chopped
4 rashers lean rindless smoked streaky bacon, chopped
1 large potato, peeled and finely diced
1 stick celery, trimmed and finely chopped
1 carrot, peeled and finely chopped
1 bay leaf
25 g (1 oz) plain flour
Pinch of saffron threads
600 ml (20 fl oz) whole milk
100 ml (3½ fl oz) double cream
Salt and freshly ground black pepper
2 tbsp freshly chopped parsley

Heat the oil in a large saucepan until very hot and add the cockles and clams. Cover and shake the pan carefully as you would for popcorn for about 1 minute. Pour in the wine, re-cover and steam the shellfish for 2–3 minutes until the shells open. Strain the shellfish through a colander or sieve, reserving the juices. Pick the flesh from about three quarters of the shellfish, discarding any that haven't opened, and set aside.

Melt the butter in another saucepan until bubbling, then stir-fry the shallots and bacon, cook stirring for about 5 minutes until softened but not browned. Add the vegetables and bay leaf, reduce the heat, cover and cook gently for 20 minutes, stirring occasionally, until the vegetables are tender. Discard the bay leaf.

Stir in the flour and cook, stirring for a further minute. Remove from the heat and add the saffron. Gradually stir in the milk and reserved cooking liquid. Return to the heat and gradually bring to the boil, stirring, and cook for 1 minute, until slightly thickened. Stir in the shellfish and cream. Heat through for a further 1–2 minutes until hot but not boiling. Taste and season as necessary. Discard the bay leaf.

To serve, ladle into large shallow soup bowls and sprinkle with chopped parsley. Serve immediately.

Mackerel in oatmeal with rhubarb sauce

When my grandparents were alive, they lived in a seaside town in Devon. We often had mackerel fresh out of the sea when we went to stay with them. Living so far inland now as I do, I'm fortunate to have a good local fishmonger who sells a variety of fresh Scottish seafood, and I'm glad to say that the mackerel is particularly good. This recipe can also be used with herrings.

Serves 4

For the sauce:
250 g (9 oz) rhubarb, trimmed and cut into 2.5cm (1in) lengths
50 g (2 oz) caster sugar
2 tbsp apple juice
1–2 tbsp raspberry vinegar
Salt

For the mackerel:
4 medium mackerel, cleaned, heads and tails removed
Salt and freshly ground black pepper
115 g (4 oz) medium oatmeal
2 tbsp sunflower oil

First make the sauce, put the rhubarb in a saucepan and add the sugar and apple juice. Heat gently until steaming, then cover and cook for 7–8 minutes until tender and soft. Stir in vinegar and salt to taste, and set aside to cool, then cover and chill until ready to serve.

For the fish, taking each fish individually, put on a board lined with clear wrap, cut-side down. Press lightly with your fingers down the middle of the back. Turn the fish over and ease up the backbone. Fold the fish in half. Season well and coat all over with oatmeal. Repeat with the remaining fish.

Heat the oil in a large frying pan and fry the fish for 4–5 minutes on each side. Drain well, cut in half and serve hot with the cold rhubarb sauce and a crisp salad.

Baked brill with pea salsa and samphire

Brill is a flat fish with meaty white flesh. A perfect accompaniment to fish at this time of year is the slightly neglected marsh samphire. This wild seashore plant grows over the mudflats below the high-tide line mostly in East Anglia. You're most likely to find it for sale in your fishmonger. It is salty and requires little cooking. Replace with fine green beans if preferred.

Serves 4

4 x 225 g (8 oz) brill fillets
Salt and freshly ground black pepper
1 tbsp plain flour
1 tbsp cold pressed rapeseed oil
150 ml (5 fl oz) dry white wine
150 ml (5 fl oz) fresh fish or vegetable stock (see page 156)
1 garlic clove, peeled and crushed
675 g (1½ lb) fresh peas, shelled
A few sprigs fresh basil
250 g (9 oz) marsh samphire
25 g (1 oz) unsalted butter
Fresh pea shoots and basil to garnish

Preheat the oven to its hottest setting. Wash and pat dry the fish, then season lightly with salt and pepper, and dust with a little flour. Heat the oil in a frying pan until hot and then sear the fillets for 1 minute on each side, until golden. Transfer to an oven proof dish and cook for about 5 minutes until tender.

Meanwhile, pour the wine and stock into a saucepan and bring to the boil. Add the garlic and peas, cover and cook for about 5 minutes until tender. Without draining, mash lightly with a potato masher. Rip up the basil and stir into the peas. Set aside to keep warm.

For the samphire, rinse thoroughly, and trim away any damaged parts and the woody ends. Bring a saucepan of water the boil, place the samphire in a steamer compartment or sieve and stand on top of the water. Cover and steam lightly for about 5 minutes, turning halfway through, until just tender. Drain and dot with butter.

To serve, divide the pea salsa between 4 warm serving plates. Top with samphire and a piece of fish. Garnish with pea shoots and fresh basil and serve with a wedge of lemon.

Crab cakes with green mayonnaise

A real American favourite, popular in coastal areas, crab cakes make a tasty change from other fish varieties. You can add whatever herbs you like to the mayonnaise, but more delicate flavours will work best with fish.

Serves 4

450 g (1 lb) cooked, mashed potatoes
1 free range egg yolk
450 g (1 lb) cooked white crab meat
3 hardboiled free range eggs, peeled and finely chopped
50 g (2 oz) gherkins, drained and finely chopped
Dash of Tabasco sauce
Salt and freshly ground black pepper
4 tbsp plain flour
115 g (4 oz) dry white breadcrumbs
25 g (1 oz) butter
4 tbsp vegetable oil

For the green mayonnaise:
1 quantity mayonnaise (see page 154)
2 tbsp freshly chopped dill
2 tbsp freshly chopped chervil
2 tbsp freshly chopped tarragon
1 tbsp wholegrain mustard
2 tsp caster sugar

Mix together the potato, egg yolk, crab meat, and chopped egg. Add Tabasco and seasoning to taste. Divide into eight portions and shape each portion into a cake about 7.5 cm (3 in) in diameter – dust the surface and your hands with flour to prevent stickiness. Place on baking parchment-lined tray and chill for at least 30 minutes.

Meanwhile, mix all the mayonnaise ingredients together, cover and chill until required.

Sprinkle the breadcrumbs on a plate and coat both sides of each crab cake in crumbs. Melt the butter with the oil in a large frying pan until bubbling and cook the crab cakes in two batches for 4-5 minutes on each side until golden and hot. Drain on kitchen paper and keep warm. Serve the crab cakes with the mayonnaise and a crisp salad.

Thick sole goujons with cucumber tartare sauce

A fine textured white flat fish, sole is best cooked simply in order to enjoy its succulent texture and fine flavour. I prefer to keep the fish in thicker strips in order to retain its juices. Cucumber is the perfect accompaniment giving texture and delicate fresh flavour.

Serves 4

For the cucumber tartare sauce:
¼ cucumber, washed and finely chopped
A few sprigs fresh tarragon, finely chopped
1 tbsp tarragon vinegar
1 tsp caster sugar
1 quantity mayonnaise (see page 154)

For the goujons:
4 x 115 g (4 oz) sole fillets
40 g (1½ oz) plain flour
Salt and freshly ground black pepper
1 large free range egg, beaten
150 g (5 oz) dry natural breadcrumbs
Sunflower oil for deep frying

First make the tartare sauce. Mix all the ingredients together, cover and chill until required.

For the goujons, wash and pat dry the fillets. Using a sharp knife, start at the tail end, slip in the knife against the skin, and slice the flesh away, keeping the skin taut. The flesh should easily come away in one piece. Alternatively, ask your fishmonger to skin the fish for you. Cut the fish into 2.5 cm (1 in) thick slices.

Sieve the flour on to a plate and season lightly. Beat the eggs with 2 tablespoons water and place on another plate. Put the breadcrumbs on another plate. Toss the fish in the flour to coat, then dip in egg and finally coat in breadcrumbs.

Heat the oil for deep-frying to 190°C (375°F). Deep-fry the fish in 3 batches for 3-4 minutes until just cooked through and lightly golden – do not over cook otherwise the fish will be dry. Drain well and keep warm whilst cooking all the fish.

To serve, divide between warm serving plates and accompany with small pots of tartare sauce for dipping. Serve with a separate crisp salad, some brown bread and butter and a squeeze of lemon. Perfect!

Halibut en croute with julienne vegetables

I've chosen slightly Oriental flavours to go with this chunky white fish, but you can keep it plainer if you prefer. Sea bass or the top-of-the-range turbot are also worth trying cooked this way.

Serves 4

2.5 cm (1 in) piece root ginger, peeled and finely shredded
2 spring onions, trimmed and finely chopped
4 tbsp freshly chopped coriander
2 tsp coriander seeds, lightly crushed
4 x 150 g (5 oz) skinless halibut fillet steaks
4 x large sheets filo pastry, thawed if frozen
25 g (1 oz) butter, melted
1 tbsp vegetable oil
225 g (8 oz) carrots, peeled and finely shredded
225 g (8 oz) courgettes, trimmed and finely shredded
2 medium leeks, trimmed, rinsed and finely shredded
Light soy sauce to season
Fresh coriander to garnish

Preheat the oven to 200°C (400°F, gas 6). Mix together the ginger, spring onion, chopped coriander and coriander seeds. Set aside. Wash and pat dry the fish steaks. Set aside.

Lay the filo sheets out on the work surface and brush with melted butter. Fold each sheet in half and brush with more butter. Divide the ginger mixture between the pastry, piling it in the centre of each piece. Lay a fish steak on top of each. Fold up the pastry sides to enclose the fish and to make a parcel.

Place the fish, folded side down, on a baking sheet lined with baking parchment. Brush with any remaining butter and bake for 20–25 minutes until golden and crisp.

Five minutes before the end of the fish cooking time, heat the oil in a wok until hot, then stir fry the vegetables for 2-3 minutes until just tender. Season with soy sauce.

To serve, pile the vegetables on to warmed serving plates and top with a piece of fish. Garnish with fresh coriander to serve.

Plaice and crab roulades en gratin

I love this combination of softly flaking white fish and the slightly salty taste of smoked salmon. It makes a great dish for entertaining and can easily be prepared a few hours in advance.

Serves 4

40 g (1½ oz) butter
40 g (1½ oz) plain flour
300 ml (10 fl oz) fresh fish stock (see page 156)
300 ml (10 fl oz) whole milk
Salt and freshly ground black pepper
4 tbsp freshly chopped dill
4 x 115 g (4 oz) skinless plaice fillets
115 g (4 oz) thinly sliced smoked salmon
50 g (2 oz) medium fat soft cheese with garlic and herbs
115 g (4 oz) cooked white crab meat
50 g (2 oz) local Cheddar-style cheese, finely grated
Fresh dill to garnish

Preheat the oven to 180°C (350°F, gas 4). Melt the butter in a saucepan, add the flour and stir with a wooden spoon until smooth. Cook over a gentle heat for 2 minutes, stirring, until bubbling. Remove from the heat and gradually stir in the stock and milk.

Return to a moderate heat, and bring to the boil, stirring continuously, taking the wooden spoon right to the edges of the pan. Once thickened, cook gently for about 3 minutes. Add seasoning to taste, and stir in the chopped dill. Set aside whilst preparing the fish.

Wash and pat dry the plaice fillets, then slice in half lengthways. Lay strips of salmon over the skinned side of each piece of plaice, trimming to fit as necessary. Mix the soft cheese and crab together and carefully spread over the salmon. Roll up as tightly as possible from the narrow, tail end.

Spoon the prepared sauce into a shallow oven proof gratin dish and smooth over evenly. Push the plaice rolls into the sauce. Cover and cook for 20 minutes. Remove the foil, sprinkle with cheese and return to the oven for a further 10 minutes until cooked through. Serve garnished with fresh dill, accompanied with freshly cooked baby vegetables and new potatoes.

Pressed tomato moulds with goat's cheese

Semi-drying tomatoes is a great way to increase their sweetness and intensity of flavour. If you don't want to use them straightaway, keep them in the fridge, submerged in a lightly flavoured oil, in a sealed container for up to 2 weeks.

Serves 4

900 g (2 lb) ripe well flavoured, small tomatoes
Salt
A few leaves fresh basil
225 g (8 oz) local log shaped goat's cheese, thinly sliced
Freshly ground black pepper
2 tbsp balsamic vinegar
2 tbsp cold pressed rapeseed oil
2 tsp locally produced clear honey
2 tbsp freshly chopped chives

Preheat the oven to its lowest setting – ideally about 60°C (120°F); it should not exceed 80°C (160°F). Line two large baking sheets with foil and place wire racks to fit on top.

Cut the tomatoes in half, sprinkle with salt and arrange cut side down on wads of absorbent kitchen paper, and set aside for 30 minutes. Place cut side down on the prepared wire racks and trays. Put in the oven, leaving the door slightly ajar if necessary to ensure the tomatoes dry rather than cook, and leave for about 8 hours, turning over after 6 hours, until slightly shrivelled and puckered, but still fleshy. Turn off the heat and allow to cool.

Stand 4 x 7 cm (3½ in) diameter, 4 cm (1½ in) deep round cake rings on a tray lined with clear wrap. Layer the cold tomatoes with a few leaves basil, slices of goat's cheese and seasoning with black pepper as you go, until all the rings are slightly overfilled. Cover with clear wrap and stand a weighted board on top of the moulds to form a press. Chill overnight.

When ready to serve, transfer each tomato mould to a serving plate and carefully remove the ring. Whisk the remaining ingredients together and drizzle over each mould to serve. Best served at room temperature for a fuller flavour. Accompany with warm crusty white bread.

Stir fried spring cabbage

A bright green leafy vegetable just destined for the wok. Stir frying is the best way to preserve its colour, vitamins and texture. At this time of the year, spring cabbage is fresh and tender, and this is a recipe designed to make the most of it.

Serves 4

500 g (1 lb 2 oz) spring cabbage
6 leaves wild garlic or 1 garlic clove, peeled and crushed
2 tbsp sunflower oil
2 tbsp dark soy sauce
2 tbsp Chinese rice wine or sweet sherry
1 tbsp clear honey
2 tbsp toasted sesame seeds

Discard any damaged outer leaves, and trim away the tough ribs and stem. Rinse in cold running water, and shake well to remove the excess water. Shred finely. If using wild garlic, wash well and shred finely.

Heat the oil in a wok or large frying pan and stir fry the cabbage and garlic for 2–3 minutes until just wilting. Add the soy sauce, rice wine and honey and continue to stir fry for a further 2–3 minutes until just tender.

Pile on to a warmed serving platter and sprinkle with sesame seeds. Serve immediately.

Pasta with spinach, blue cheese, pine nuts and raisins

This is one of my favourite pasta sauces and it's so easy to make. Investigate local cheeses for this recipe, just about any blue cheese will be OK, the tastier the better!

Serves 4

450 g (1 lb) pasta shapes
Salt and freshly ground black pepper
50 g (2 oz) unsalted butter
600 g (1 lb 5 oz) young leaf spinach
225 g (8 oz) local blue cheese
8 tbsp double cream
40 g (1½ oz) seedless raisins
¼ tsp ground nutmeg
50 g (2 oz) toasted pine nuts

Bring a large saucepan of lightly salted water to the boil and cook the pasta according to the manufacturer's instructions until 'al dente' – just cooked, but still slightly firm. Drain well, return to the pan and toss in the butter.

Meanwhile, wash the spinach thoroughly and remove any large stalks. Place in a clean saucepan whilst still wet, then cover and cook, stirring occasionally, over a medium heat for 5–6 minutes until just wilted. Drain well using a colander or sieve, pressing against the sides to squeeze out the excess liquid.

Break the cheese into small pieces and place in a saucepan with the cream and raisins. Heat gently until melted to a creamy sauce. Stir in the drained spinach, black pepper and ground nutmeg.

To serve, toss the pasta in the sauce and pile into warmed serving bowls. Sprinkle with more black pepper and nutmeg if liked and scatter a few pine nuts over the top to serve.

Spring vegetable frittata

You can put just about anything into this thick baked omelette, and it's also a good way of using up leftover vegetables. Cook the fresh vegetables lightly beforehand so that the egg stays softly firm and doesn't overcook. I prefer to sprinkle chopped herbs over the finished dish, but you can add them to the beaten egg if you prefer.

Serves 4

115 g (4 oz) small broccoli florets
115 g (4 oz) small cauliflower florets
115 g (4 oz) asparagus, trimmed and cut into 2.5 cm (1 in) lengths
115 g (4 oz) baby carrots, trimmed and halved lengthways
115 g (4 oz) new potatoes, scrubbed and sliced
25 g (1 oz) butter
1 tbsp sunflower oil
1 medium leek, trimmed and sliced
Salt and freshly ground black pepper
8 large free range eggs, beaten
Assorted fragrant chopped herbs like chervil, tarragon, chives and fennel to garnish

Preheat the oven to 190°C (375°F, gas 5). Bring a saucepan of water to the boil. Place all the vegetables except the leek in a steamer compartment or large sieve and stand over the water. Cover and steam for 15–20 minutes, turning occasionally, until just tender but not soft. Remove from the water and set aside.

Meanwhile, melt the butter with the oil in a large frying pan, and when bubbling, add the leek and stir-fry over a medium heat for 3–4 minutes until softened but not browned. Add the vegetables and cook, stirring, for about a minute until the vegetables are coated in the leek. Transfer to a greased 25-cm (10-in) round baking dish.

Season the eggs and pour evenly over the vegetables. Bake in the oven for about 30 minutes until lightly golden and just set. Stand for 10 minutes, then cut into wedges and serve scattered with chopped fresh herbs.

Pea tarts

I first discovered a variation of this pastry when I was researching recipes for a Cuban cook book. Cream cheese makes a short and slightly flaky pastry which is an absolute joy to eat with fresh spring vegetables like peas. Artichoke hearts, beans and courgettes would also make suitable fillings.

Makes 6

For the pastry:
300 g (10 oz) plain flour
Pinch of salt
175 g (6 oz) unsalted butter
175 g (6 oz) full fat soft cheese

For the filling:
500 g (1 lb 2 oz) fresh peas, shelled
2 free range eggs, beaten
150 ml (5 fl oz) double cream
4 spring onions, trimmed and white and green parts finely chopped

First make the pastry. Sift the flour and salt into a bowl and rub in the butter. Bind together with the soft cheese, then knead gently on a lightly floured surface. Wrap and chill for an hour.

Meanwhile, bring a saucepan of water to the boil and blanch the peas for 2 minutes. Drain well and rinse in cold water. Set aside in cold water. Preheat the oven to 220°C (425°F, gas 7).

Divide the pastry in to 6. On a lightly floured surface, gently roll out into 6 roughly shaped 20-cm (8-in) circles. Drain the peas well and pat dry with absorbent kitchen paper. Carefully pile the peas on to the centre of each pastry circle and bring up the sides of the pastry, pinching together to enclose the peas and make a rough case, but leaving the top open.

Transfer to a baking parchment lined baking tray. Beat the eggs together with the cream, spring onions and plenty of seasoning, and pour in to each pie. Bake for about 25 minutes until golden. Stand for 10 minutes before serving, hot or cold.

Broad bean falafels

If you like Middle Eastern cuisine, falafels will be well known to you. They are often made with chick peas, but in Egypt, falafels are made with dried broad beans. This recipe uses fresh beans so they are bright green when you bite in to them, and full of sweet beany flavour. It also works well with fresh peas.

Makes 8

1 kg (2 lb 3½ oz) fresh broad beans, shelled
Salt and freshly ground black pepper
1 tsp cumin seeds, lightly crushed
½ tsp baking powder
1 clove garlic, peeled
15 g (½ oz) fresh coriander
15 g (½ oz) fresh parsley
4 spring onions, trimmed and white and green parts roughly chopped
2 tbsp gram (chickpea) flour, plus extra for dusting
150 ml (5 fl oz) sunflower oil, for shallow frying

Bring a saucepan of water to the boil and add the beans, bring back to the boil and blanch for 1 minute only. Drain and rinse in cold water. Drain well and allow to air dry for 10 minutes.

Put the beans in a blender or food processor and blend until they form a very smooth, soft paste. Transfer to a bowl and season well. Stir in the cumin seeds and baking powder. Cover and let stand for 1 hour.

Put the garlic, coriander, parsley and spring onions in a blender or food processor and blend for a few seconds to form a well minced green paste, and stir into the bean mixture along with 2 Tbsp gram flour.

Divide into 8 portions and pile in mounds on to a board lined with baking parchment. Chill for 30 minutes.

Carefully press into patty shapes and dust lightly with extra gram flour. Heat the oil in a medium frying pan until hot and fry 4 falafels at a time, for 6–7 minutes, turning once, until they are crisp and brown. Drain well and keep warm.

Serve warm with sweet tomatoes and wedges of lemon to squeeze over.

Note: Traditionally falafel are served with tahini sauce – a paste made from sesame seeds, diluted with water and lemon juice, and seasoned with salt and pepper.

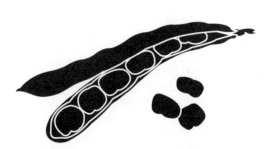

Asparagus envelopes

Fine asparagus works best for this recipe, but if you have the thicker stems, cut them in half lengthways. I've wrapped the bundles in bacon, but you can leave this out if you prefer a vegetarian version.

Serves 4

300 g (10 oz) puff pastry, thawed if frozen
20 fine asparagus spears
4 rashers rindless unsmoked streaky bacon
Freshly ground black pepper
1 tsp cold pressed rapeseed oil
1 free range egg, beaten

Preheat the oven to 220°C (425°F, gas 7). Roll out the pastry on a lightly floured surface to a 30-cm (12-in) square, and cut into four smaller squares.

Trim the asparagus to 15-cm (6-in) lengths – use the stalks for soups or risottos. Divide into four equal sized bundles, and wrap each in a rasher of bacon. Lay on the pastry square in a diagonal. Season with black pepper

Bring up two opposite sides of pastry, and press together on top of bundle. Transfer to a baking tray lined with baking parchment, and brush the asparagus with oil. Brush the pastry with egg and bake in the oven for about 25 minutes until golden and tender. Best served warm.

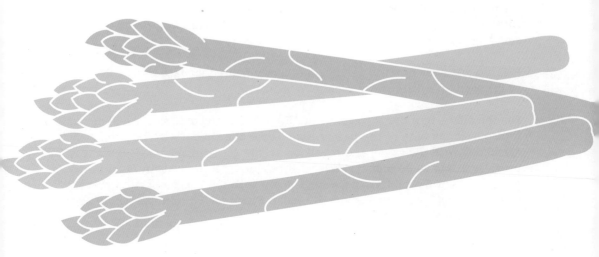

My Granny's rhubarb pie

My maternal grandparents used to grow the best rhubarb I've ever tasted – a variety called champagne. It was so tangy that it would make your tongue tingle. This is my version of the pie Granny would make to serve their favourite home-grown fruit at its best.

Serves 6–8

For the pastry:
250 g (9 oz) plain flour
75 g (3 oz) butter, cut into small pieces
75 g (3 oz) lard, cut into small pieces
3 tbsp caster sugar
Approx. 3 tbsp cold water

For the filling:
1 tbsp cornflour
150 g (5 oz) + 2 tbsp caster sugar
450 g (1 lb) thin rhubarb stalks, trimmed and cut into 2.5 cm (1 in) pieces
1 free range egg white, beaten

Preheat the oven to 200°C (400°F, gas 6). Sieve the flour into a bowl and rub in the butter and lard until well blended. Stir in the sugar and bind together with sufficient cold water to bring the mixture together. Knead lightly to form a smooth dough. Wrap and chill for 30 minutes.

Roll out just over half the pastry on a lightly floured surface to fit a 20-cm (8-in) round pie dish or tin, 4 cm (1½ in) deep.

For the filling, mix the cornflour and 150 g (5 oz) sugar together and sprinkle 2 tbsp over the base of the pastry case. Layer the rhubarb in the pastry shell sprinkling with the sugar and cornflour as you go. Transfer to a baking tray, brush with egg white and sprinkle with remaining 2 tbsp sugar. Bake in the oven for about 50 minutes, covering the top with foil if necessary to prevent over-browning, until the rhubarb is tender. Stand for 15 minutes before serving hot or cold with custard or clotted cream.

Rhubarb fool crème brûlées

A sophisticated version of rhubarb and custard. Using raw rhubarb means that you get more flavour, but you will have a separation between fruit and custard, and therefore, they will take longer to cook than other brulées.

Makes 6

600 ml (20 fl oz) whipping cream
2 vanilla pods, split lengthways
225 g (8 oz) even-sized rhubarb stalks
225 g (8 oz) caster sugar
4 free range egg yolks

Preheat the oven to 150°C (300°F, gas 2). Heat the whipping cream in a saucepan until just below boiling point. Remove from the heat and add the vanilla pods. Set aside to infuse for 30 minutes. Discard the pods.

Trim the rhubarb, and cut into 2.5 cm (1 in) long pieces. Divide between 6 ramekin dishes, and sprinkle each with two tsp sugar. Stand the dishes in a roasting tin.

Whisk 50 g (2 oz) sugar with the egg yolks until thick and pale and whisk in the infused cream. Divide between the ramekins. Pour in enough hot water to come halfway up the sides. Bake for about 1 hour 15 minutes until just set. Note: the rhubarb will probably rise to the top and the juices and sugar will form a syrup underneath the custard. Remove from the water and allow to cool, then chill for at least 2 hours.

Sprinkle with the remaining sugar and place under a preheated hot grill for 4-5 minutes until melted and caramelised. Cool, and then chill for a further 2 hours. Stand at room temperature for about 20 minutes before serving.

Gooseberry cheesecake

Gooseberries have been used in British cooking since Tudor times, and the early varieties are usually ready by the end of May if weather conditions suit. The tart, green gooseberries are best for this recipe, but if you prefer the sweeter varieties, reduce the sugar content accordingly.

Serves 8–10

500 g (1 lb 2 oz) green gooseberries, topped and tailed
approx. 150 g (5 oz) caster sugar
2 heads elderflowers, washed (optional)
6 tbsp cold water
175 g (6 oz) oaty biscuits, finely crushed
65 g (2½ oz) butter, melted
5 sheets of leaf gelatine
225 g (8 oz) full fat soft cheese
150 ml (5 fl oz) double cream

Grease and line an 20-cm (8-in) spring clip cake tin. Place the gooseberries in a saucepan with 115 g (4 oz) sugar and the elderflowers, if using. Add 2 tbsp water, bring to the boil, cover and simmer for 6–8 minutes until soft and pulpy. Discard the elderflower. Push through a nylon sieve to make a smooth purée – approx. 350 ml (12 fl oz). Set aside to cool.

Mix the crushed biscuits together with the melted butter and press into the base of the prepared tin. Chill until required.

Cut each leaf of gelatine into small pieces and place in a bowl. Spoon over 4 tbsp cold water and leave aside to soak for 10 minutes. Melt the gelatine over a pan of simmering water, and set aside to cool.

Place the soft cheese in a mixing bowl and stir in the gooseberry purée and remaining sugar to taste. In another bowl whip the cream until just peaking and fold into the gooseberries and soft cheese. Carefully fold the gelatine into the cheese mixture. Pile on top of the base and smooth the top. Chill for at least 4 hours until set. Unclip the tin and transfer the cheesecake to a serving plate – looks lovely decorated with washed sprays of elderflowers.

Elderflower sorbet

The elder tree flowers in late Spring and its delicately perfumed white flower clusters offer a delicious floral flavouring. They also combine well with fruits such as apples, pears, strawberries and gooseberries.

Serves 4

125 g (4½ oz) caster sugar
450 ml (15 fl oz) water
Thinly pared rind and juice 1 small lemon
50g (2 oz) or 2 large heads elderflowers
1 free range egg white

First make the sugar syrup. Place the sugar in a large saucepan and pour over the water. Add the lemon rind and heat, stirring, until the sugar dissolves. Raise the heat, bring to the boil and simmer, without stirring, for 5 minutes. Remove from the heat, add the elderflowers and lemon juice and allow to cool completely. Strain and set aside.

Pour the cold syrup in to a freezer-proof container. Freeze until just beginning to set round the edges – approx. 1½–2 hours. Whisk well to break down the ice crystals evenly. Whisk the egg white and fold into the slushy syrup. Return to the freezer and freeze for a further 1½–2 hours, whisking every 30 minutes, until firm. Cover and store in the freezer until required.

To serve, stand the sorbet at room temperature for about 20 minutes until soft enough to scoop. Scoop in to serving glasses and serve immediately.

Easter meringue nests with chocolate-dipped strawberries

Whether you serve this as a dessert for Easter lunch, or a tea time treat, you're bound to be popular. Chocolate goes so well with sweet British strawberries. Use milk chocolate if preferred.

Makes 4

2 free range egg whites
100 g (3½ oz) caster sugar
A few drops vanilla extract
4 Tsp cocoa powder
150 g (5 oz) plain chocolate, broken into pieces
175 g (6 oz) small whole strawberries, washed
100 ml (3½ fl oz) double cream, at room temperature

Preheat the oven to 130°C (250°F, gas ½). In a large grease-free bowl, whisk the egg whites until very stiff and dry. Whisk in half the sugar. Fold in the remaining sugar and vanilla extract carefully using a large metal spoon.

Sift the cocoa on top of the meringue mixture and gently marble it through, taking care not to fold it in completely. Pile in to 4 mounds on to a large baking sheet lined with baking parchment, and smooth off the sides using the back of a spoon, and make an indent in each to form a nest shape. Bake on the bottom shelf of the oven for 2½–3 hours until the meringues are firm – prop the oven door open slightly if they start to over-colour. Switch off the heat and leave to cool in the oven.

Place 50 g (2 oz) chocolate pieces in a heatproof bowl over a pan of gently simmering water and allow to melt. Remove from the water and holding each strawberry by the stalk, half dip in the chocolate. Place on a board lined with baking parchment to set, and chill until required.

When ready to serve, melt the remaining chocolate as above and set aside to cool until slightly warm – about 30 minutes cooling.

Whilst whisking the chocolate, gradually pour over the cream, whisking until thickly whipped and glossy. Transfer to a piping bag fitted with a 1 cm (½ in) star nozzle and pipe the cream into each meringue nest. Top with a few strawberries. Serve with the remaining strawberries.

Note: If chilled, the meringue will start to dissolve.

Extra indulgent cream tea scones and jam

One of life's pleasures surely is sitting outside on a sunny day in the shade of a leafy tree tucking into a cream tea. Having Devonian grandparents, we were used to homemade scones, thick Devonshire clotted cream and home grown strawberry jam. This is my version of scones and a super speedy fresh strawberry 'jam' packed full of fruity flavour.

Serves 4

For the scones:
225 g (8 oz) self raising flour
1 tsp baking powder
50 g (2 oz) ground almonds
50 g (2 oz) caster sugar
75 g (3 oz) butter, cut into small pieces
Approx. 125 ml (4 fl oz) whole milk

For the 'jam':
225 g (8 oz) ripe strawberries
2–3 tbsp vanilla sugar

Clotted cream to serve

Preheat the oven to 220°C (425°F, gas 7). First make the scones. Sieve the flour and baking powder into a bowl. Stir in the almonds and caster sugar. Rub in the butter until well blended and then gradually add sufficient milk, mixing until the ingredients form together to make a softish dough. Turn on to a lightly floured surface and knead gently until smooth. Divide into 4 equal pieces and shape each one into a round about 2.5 cm (1 in) thick. Transfer to a lightly greased baking sheet and bake in the oven for 15–18 minutes until risen and lightly golden. Transfer to a wire rack to cool for 30 minutes.

Meanwhile, hull the strawberries, wash well and pat dry. Mash using a fork and place in a serving bowl. Stir in vanilla sugar to taste, then cover and stand at room temperature to allow the flavours to develop.

Serve the scones whilst warm, split in half. Add a good dollop of clotted cream to each half and spoon over the strawberry jam to serve. Delicious!

Without doubt, this is the most colourful and tasty time of the year for food. With such a huge variety of British ingredients to choose from, it takes little effort to rustle up a truly sensational meal in next to no time.

SUMMER

(beginning of June, through
July, to the end of August)

First of all there are all the crisp salad vegetables and flavoursome herbs to choose from alongside sweet ripe tomatoes, peppers, aubergines, courgettes, marrows, runner beans, sweet corn, the list is endless. One of the prime vegetables, the globe artichoke, makes a big impression in Summer – it looks a bit daunting, but once prepared, it has a unique delicate flavour that can't be matched.

Of course, soft fruits are at their peak during these months. Jewels of black, green, purple, red and pink shine out from small punnets on every greengrocer's stall. Perfect to eat on their own as a simple dessert, but also easy to mix with other ingredients in baking, creams, cheesecakes and ices. If you have a glut of home grown produce it is worth setting aside some time to preserve the fruits of your labours so that you can enjoy them later in the year. I've included several recipes for jam and jelly making, as well as less traditional methods of preserving like freezing.

If you're eating out of doors, most likely you'll be setting up the barbecue, and a lot of seasonal produce cooks very well with a smoky edge. Fresh sardines are perfect for cooking outdoors and eating on a Summer's evening, and they cook quickly over hot coals; salmon steaks are also good, and cubes of chunky fish like monkfish are sweet and juicy if wrapped in bacon and cooked on skewers – see page 58 for recipe. Chicken and pork are obvious barbecue meats, but why not try cooking the small game bird, quail, for something a bit different – lightly seasoned and well basted, they make an easy to eat and very delicious addition to the usual barbecue fare – check out my recipe on page 52.

Incidentally, just when we're all enjoying the height of Summer sunshine (hopefully!), we have a subtle reminder of the months ahead, when the 12th August heralds the start of the game season with the first grouse shoots. But for the meantime, let's enjoy this time of the year a little longer with a full list of British produce around in June, July and August.

Apples (dessert): George Cave/ Discovery/ Worcester/ Pearmain/ Egremont Russet	new season from August to October
Asparagus	until July
Aubergine (homegrown)	harvest July to October
Beans: broad	new season June and July
outdoors	new season June to September
runner	new season July to October
kidney	new season from June to November
Blackberries (Brambles)	new season from July to October
Blackcurrants & redcurrants (& whitecurrants)	new season from June to August
Blueberries	new season mid-July to September
Cabbages: Summer	new season from June to October
Savoy	new season from August to May
Red	new season from August to January
Winter	new season from August to March
Celery	new season from June to February
Cherries	new season from June to August
Courgettes	new season from June to September
Cucumber	all year at best in late Summer
Damsons	new season from August to October
Endive	until August
Globe artichoke	new season from June to September
Gooseberries	until August
Greengages	new season from July to August
Kohlrabi	new season from July to March
Leeks	new season from August to May
Marrows	new season from June to October
Nectarines	new season from June to September
Onions (pickling)	new season from July to December
Peaches	new season from June to September
Pears: Comice, Conference and Williams	new season from August to March
Peas	
Peppers (homegrown)	harvest from July to September
Plums	new season from June to October
Potatoes: maincrop	new season from August onwards
new	until July
Pumpkin & Squash	new season from August to December
Raspberries	new season from June to September
Rhubarb (outdoor)	until end of June
Spinach	
Strawberries (outdoor)	
Sweetcorn	new season from August to October
Tomatoes	
Wild mushrooms	new season from August to November

MEAT: lamb, duck, hare. 12th August – grouse season begins
FISH: crab, Dover sole, halibut, herring, lemon sole, lobster, monkfish, plaice, salmon, sardines, sea bass, sea trout

Smoky sweet corn chowder

Fresh corn on the cob, dripping with butter, is quite a sensuous food experience. This thick soup gives you all the pleasure but without the mess!

Serves 4

4 ripe corn on the cobs
1 tsp caster sugar
40 g (1½ oz) butter
1 large onion, peeled and finely chopped
1 large potato, peeled and finely diced
1 bay leaf
25 g (1 oz) plain flour
600 ml (20 fl oz) whole milk
300 ml (10 fl oz) fresh chicken or vegetable stock (see page 156)
4 tbsp double cream
Salt and freshly ground black pepper
2 tsp sweet smoked paprika
2 tbsp freshly chopped parsley

Strip off the outer leaves and silky strings from the sweet corn. Bring a saucepan of water to the boil, add the sugar but no salt and cook about 8 minutes – salt will toughen the kernels. Test for 'doneness' by pricking carefully with a skewer to see if the kernels are tender. Rinse in cold running water to cool, then strip off the kernels by running a small sharp knife down the length of the cob, collecting the kernels as they are released. Set aside.

Melt the butter in a large saucepan, add the onion and cook for 5 minutes until softened but not browned. Add the potatoes and bay leaf and cook, stirring, for 1 minute, then reduce the heat, cover the pan, and cook gently for about 20 minutes, stirring occasionally, until just tender. Stir in the flour and cook, stirring for a further minute. Remove from the heat and gradually stir in the milk and stock. Bring to the boil, stirring, for 1 minute until slightly thickened. Cool for 10 minutes. Discard the bay leaf. Strain the cooking liquid, reserving the vegetables.

Put half the sweet corn in a blender or food processor and add the strained liquid. Blend for a few seconds until smooth. Return to the saucepan. Add the remaining sweet corn, reserved vegetables, cream, seasoning and smoked paprika. Gently heat through for 2–3 minutes without boiling until piping hot. Ladle in to warm soup bowls and sprinkle with parsley to serve.

Note: Sweet corn is even more delicious cooked over the barbecue. Strip away a few leaves allowing sufficient to keep the kernels covered, and remove the silky strings. Secure the remaining leaves with string, and then blanch for 4 minutes. Drain well. Cook over the barbecue, turning frequently, for about 5-6 minutes until tender. Allow to cool, then remove the string and leaves, and strip as described above.

Soupe de poisson

This recipe is one of the best for fish lovers. It is full of the flavours of white fish at its prime. In France, a soup like this is traditionally accompanied with a spicy mayonnaise called 'rouille'. Serve with toasted rounds of French bread as well.

Serves 6

900 g (2 lb) assorted white skinless fish fillets such as cod, haddock, hake, ling, monkfish, plaice and sea bass, cut into 2 cm (¾ in) chunks
3 tbsp cold pressed rapeseed oil
1 large onion, peeled and chopped
1 large carrot, peeled and chopped
1 bulb fennel, trimmed and chopped
4 garlic cloves, peeled and chopped
1 bay leaf
1 sprig thyme
1 sprig rosemary
675 g (1½ lb) ripe tomatoes, skinned, seeded and chopped
300 ml (10 fl oz) dry white wine
Salt and freshly ground black pepper
4 tbsp Pernod
25 g (1 oz) flat leaf parsley, chopped

For the rouille:
1 quantity mayonnaise (see page 154)
1–2 tsp harissa paste or red chilli paste
2 garlic cloves, peeled and chopped
6 anchovy fillets in oil, drained
1 tbsp lemon juice
1 tbsp tomato purèe

Wash and pat dry the fish, and divide in to two equal batches; cover and chill one batch until required.

Heat the oil in a large saucepan until hot and gently fry the onion, carrot, fennel and garlic, stirring, for 5 minutes, without browning. Add the bay leaf, thyme and rosemary, stir in the tomatoes and wine. Bring to the boil and simmer for 5 minutes. Add one batch of white fish, pour in sufficient cold water to just cover the fish, bring to the boil, reduce the heat, cover and simmer gently for 20 minutes. Stand for 10 minutes, discard the herbs, then transfer to a blender or food processor and blend until smooth.

Meanwhile, make up the rouille. Place all the ingredients in a blender or food processor and blend until smooth. Cover and chill until required.

When ready to serve, put the puréed fish soup back in a saucepan, season well and bring to the boil. Add the second batch of white fish and just enough water to cover. Cover and simmer gently for 5 minutes until all the fish is cooked through. Add the Pernod, taste and season accordingly.

Ladle into warm, deep soup bowls, sprinkle generously with parsley and serve immediately each with a dollop of rouille and some toasted bread.

Moussaka

This recipe reminds me of happy times in the Med, and is, therefore, a true taste of Summer. Hothouse aubergines will be ripe and ready for picking in mid-late Summer, and this recipe makes the most of their meaty texture.

Serves 4

900 g (2 lb) aubergines
7 tbsp cold pressed rapeseed oil
2 garlic cloves, peeled and finely
   chopped
2 onions, peeled and chopped
450 g (1 lb) lean minced lamb
½ tsp ground cinnamon
1 tbsp freshly chopped oregano
675 g (1½ lb) ripe tomatoes, peeled,
   seeded and chopped
Freshly ground black pepper
2 tbsp tomato purée
50 g (2 oz) butter
50 g (2 oz) plain flour
600 ml (20 fl oz) whole milk
1 free range egg yolk
4 tbsp freshly grated local Parmesan-
   type cheese

Trim and thinly slice the aubergines to a thickness of 6 mm (¼ in). Layer up in a colander, sprinkling each layer with salt as you go. Set aside to drain over 30 minutes. Rinse well and pat dry with kitchen paper.

Heat 6 Tbsp oil in a large frying pan and gently fry the aubergines in several batches for 5–6 minutes until softened and lightly brown on each side. Drain and set aside.

Meanwhile, heat the remaining oil in a saucepan and gently fry the garlic, onion and lamb for 5 minutes, stirring, until browned all over. Add the cinnamon, oregano, tomatoes, black pepper and tomato purée. Bring to the boil, reduce the heat and simmer gently for about 40 minutes until tender and thickened.

Meanwhile, make up the white sauce. Melt the butter in a saucepan and stir in the flour. Cook for 1 minute then remove from the heat and gradually blend in the milk. Return to the heat and stir until the sauce thickens to a pouring consistency. Remove from the heat and stir in the egg yolk. Season lightly and set aside. Preheat the oven to 180°C (350°F, gas 4).

Arrange the aubergines in the base of a 5 cm (2 in) deep gratin dish. Season with pepper and top with the lamb mixture. Spoon the sauce over the top and sprinkle with cheese. Place on a baking tray and bake in the oven for 50 minutes. Leave to stand for 10 minutes, then serve with crusty bread and salad.

Ham, chicken and leek picnic pie

August is the height of the picnic season, and a pie is always popular because it's a very portable food.

Serves 8–10

For the pastry:
500 g (1 lb 2oz) plain flour
½ tsp salt
115 g (4 oz) unsalted butter
75 g (3 oz) lard
200 ml (7 fl oz) water

For the filling:
675 g (1½ lb) smoked ham, finely diced
300 g (10 oz) boneless, skinless, chicken breast, finely diced or minced
4 tbsp fresh chicken stock (see page 156)
1 tbsp freshly chopped sage
Salt and freshly ground black pepper
½ tsp ground nutmeg
2 medium leeks, trimmed and finely chopped
1 free range egg, beaten

For the jelly:
2 sheets fine leaf gelatine
200 ml (7 fl oz) cold fresh chicken stock (see page 156)

Sieve the flour and salt into a heatproof bowl and make a well in the centre. Put the butter, lard and water in a saucepan and heat gently to melt, then allow to simmer. Pour into the well and mix to form a smooth dough. Knead on a lightly floured surface, then place back in the bowl, cover and allow to stand in a warm place for about 30 minutes – don't allow the dough to go cold.

Preheat the oven to 200°C (400°F, gas 6). Grease the base and sides of a 28 x 10 x 7.5 cm (11 x 4 x 3 in) terrine tin. Place the ham and chicken in a bowl and mix in 4 tbsp chicken stock, seasoning, nutmeg and sage. Set aside. Cut off one third of the pastry and set aside. Roll out the remaining pastry on a lightly floured surface to fit the base and sides of the tin and gently press into place. Spoon half of the meat mixture into the pastry case and top with the leeks. Spoon over the remaining meat mixture and pack down well. Fold over the overhanging pastry and trim to neaten the excess.

Roll out the remaining pastry to fit the top of the tin. Brush the pie edges with beaten egg and place the lid on top. Trim and pinch down to seal. Cut out a small round from the centre of the lid and place a greased pie funnel or nozzle in the cavity. Glaze the pie with egg and place on a baking tray. Bake in the oven for 30 minutes. Reduce the temperature to 190°C (375°F, gas 5) and cook for a further 1¼ hours until richly golden – cover with foil if it browns too quickly. Stand for 15 minutes, then carefully loosen from the sides of the tin.

Cut each leaf of gelatine into small pieces and place in a bowl. Spoon over 2 tbsp stock and leave aside to soak for 10 minutes. Melt the gelatine over a pan of simmering water. Gradually pour the jelly through the funnel into the opening of the hot pie, allowing the jelly to settle after each pour. Allow to cool completely then chill overnight. The next day, release the pie from the tin and stand at room temperature for 30 minutes before slicing.

Ratatouille-stuffed pork

You can serve this pork dish as a light hot meal with vegetables, or sliced and served cold as part of a buffet or salad. The Summery flavours of the Mediterranean vegetables shine through making this perfect for the season.

Serves 4

1 small onion, peeled and finely chopped
1 small yellow pepper, deseeded and finely chopped
1 small courgette, trimmed and finely chopped
1 baby aubergine, trimmed and finely chopped
400 g (14 oz) ripe tomatoes, skinned, seeded and chopped
2 tbsp tomato purée
1 tbsp freshly chopped rosemary
Salt and freshly ground black pepper
450 g (1 lb) piece pork fillet, trimmed of fat
4 rashers rindless lean unsmoked back bacon

Preheat the oven to 190°C (375°F, gas 5). Place the vegetables in a saucepan with the tomatoes, tomato purée, rosemary and seasoning. Bring to the boil, cover and simmer for 10 minutes until tender and thick. Set aside to cool.

Wash and pat dry the pork fillet. Slice the fillet lengthwise to within 1 cm (½ in) of the other side. Place on a board and flatten with a meat mallet or cling film wrapped rolling pin, to a thickness of about 6 mm (¼ in). Cover and chill until required.

Once the vegetable mixture is cool, spread over the pork and roll up. Carefully wrap the bacon around to secure the pork together, and tie with clean pieces of string. Place in a roasting tin and bake for 35–40 minutes until tender and cooked through. To serve, discard the string, and cut into slices. Serve hot or cold, accompanied with vegetables or salad.

Coronation chicken with fresh peach salsa

An old fashioned chicken salad that's stood the test of time. It's pretty rich so it's usually accompanied with exotic fruits like mangoes or bananas. Now that peaches are at their best, they make the ideal British choice.

Serves 6

150 ml (5 fl oz) whipping cream
150 ml (5 fl oz) mayonnaise (see page 154)
4 tbsp mango or peach chutney
1 tbsp mild curry paste
675 g (1½ lb) cooked, skinless, boneless chicken, cut into bite-sized pieces
Salt and freshly ground black pepper
Assorted fresh salads leaves to serve
A few sprigs fresh coriander, chopped
50 g (2 oz) roasted cashew nuts

For the salsa:
4 ripe peaches, washed, halved, stoned and chopped
1 small red onion, peeled and finely chopped
1 tbsp white wine vinegar
1 tbsp sunflower oil
2 tsp caster sugar
½ tsp cumin seeds, lightly crushed
2 tbsp freshly chopped coriander

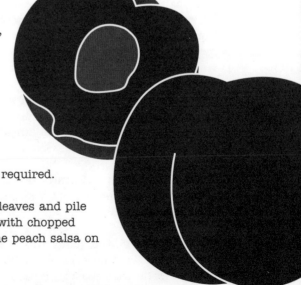

Lightly whip the cream until just peaking, then fold in the mayonnaise, chutney and curry paste to make a rich sauce. Season to taste then toss in the chicken meat and coat well. Cover and chill for at least an hour to allow the flavours to develop.

Meanwhile, make the salsa. Mix all the ingredients together, cover and chill until required.

To serve, line a serving dish with lettuce leaves and pile the chicken mayonnaise on top. Sprinkle with chopped coriander and cashews, and serve with the peach salsa on the side.

Barbecued quail with fragrant spices and sweet pepper relish

These little game birds are just right for barbecue cooking because they cook through quickly and make succulent little morsels flavoured with this aromatic spice mixture.

Serves 4

4 quails
4 tbsp cold pressed rapeseed oil
1 tsp fennel seeds, lightly crushed
1 tsp coriander seeds, lightly crushed
¼ tsp ground star anise
Salt and freshly ground black pepper

For the relish:
2 red peppers, halved and deseeded
2 yellow peppers, halved and deseeded
1 tbsp cold pressed rapeseed oil
1 onion, peeled and chopped
1 garlic clove, peeled and finely chopped
2 tbsp white wine vinegar
1 tbsp caster sugar

Put each quail breast-side down on a board lined with baking parchment, and cut along either side of the backbone. Turn the bird over and flatten out with a meat mallet or a rolling pin wrapped in clear wrap. Place the quails in a shallow dish. Mix the oil with the spices but not the seasoning and pour over the quails. Cover and chill for 2 hours.

Meanwhile, make the relish preheat the grill to its hottest setting. Lie the peppers skin side up on a grill rack and cook for 4–5 minutes until the skin blackens and blisters. Remove from the grill and place in a shallow heatproof dish. Immediately lay clear wrap directly on the blistered skin and set aside until cool enough to handle. Peel away the skin then chop the flesh finely, and place in a heatproof bowl.

Heat the oil until hot and gently fry the onion and garlic for about 5 minutes, stirring, until softened but not browned. Stir into the peppers along with the vinegar and sugar. Mix well, allow to cool, then cover and chill until required.

When ready to cook the quails, drain them from the marinade and cook over hot coals for 5-7 minutes on each side, basting occasionally with any remaining marinade. Drain well, season on each side and serve with the pepper relish.

Piri piri pork with chilli dressing

If you like garlic and chillies, then this is the dish for you. It's Portuguese in origin and can be used for fish, chicken, beef and shellfish. Start the preparation the day before for maximum flavour. The dressing will keep in a sealed container in the fridge for about a month.

Serves 4

675 g (1½ lb) lean pork fillet
2 garlic, cloves, peeled and crushed
2 tbsp cold pressed rapeseed oil

For the dressing:
2 red chillies
1 tsp coarse sea salt
150 ml (5 fl oz) cold pressed rapeseed oil
3 tbsp white wine vinegar

Slice the pork fillet into 5 cm (2 in) long thin strips and place in a shallow dish. Stir in the garlic and 2 tbsp oil. Cover and chill overnight.

Meanwhile, make the dressing, halve the chillies and remove the stalks. Chop the flesh along with the seeds and place in a small, screw-top jar. Add the salt, oil and vinegar. Seal, shake well and store at room temperature overnight.

The next day, preheat the grill to a medium setting. Drain the pork, discarding the marinade, and arrange, well spaced out, in a shallow heatproof dish. Cook for 6–7 minutes, turning occasionally, until the meat is cooked through and lightly golden.

To serve, shake the dressing, and pour into a small serving bowl. Serve the pork hot with the dressing to dip into.

Seafood rice

You can use whatever seafood is in season depending on when you cook the dish – mussels, langoustines, crab and lobster can be added, as can chunks of firm white fish. The chorizo adds a spiciness to the dish, but you can leave it out if you prefer.

Serves 4

2 tbsp cold pressed rapeseed oil
115 g (4 oz) chorizo sausage, finely chopped
1 large onion, peeled and finely chopped
2 garlic clove, peeled and finely chopped
2 red peppers, deseeded and sliced
250 g (9 oz) Valencia rice
Good pinch of saffron
1 bay leaf
Salt and freshly ground black pepper
600 ml (20 fl oz) fresh fish stock (see page 156)
300 ml (10 fl oz) dry white wine
225 g (8 oz) small clams, cleaned thoroughly
225 g (8 oz) cockles, scrubbed and well rinsed
225 g (8 oz) queen scallops, washed
225 g (8 oz) peeled shrimps
2 Tbsp freshly chopped parsley

Heat the oil in a large frying pan until hot and gently fry the chorizo, onion, garlic and peppers for 5 minutes, without browning. Add the rice, and cook, stirring, for 1 minute, to coat the rice in the mixture.

Add the saffron, bay leaf and seasoning. Pour over the stock and wine. Bring to the boil, simmer gently for 15 minutes, stirring occasionally, until reduced. Add the seafood, mix in well, then cover the pan and cook gently for 5 minutes until the shells open, and the rice has absorbed most of the liquid. Remove from the heat and stand covered for 10 minutes.

Discard the bay leaf and any shells that haven't opened. Sprinkle with chopped parsley and serve straight from the pan.

Baked sea bass with fragrant herbs and fennel

Cooking fish in parchment means that all the juices stay in the parcel and help keep the fish succulent and tasty. Choose herbs that are mildy flavoured for this dish so that they don't overpower the finished dish.

Serves 4

4 x 150 g (5 oz) sea bass fillets, scaled
Salt and freshly ground black pepper
Juice ½ lemon
2 bulbs fennel, trimmed and finely sliced
4 sprigs dill
4 sprigs tarragon
4 sprigs chervil
2 tbsp cold pressed rapeseed oil
Fresh herbs to garnish

Preheat the oven to 200°C (400°F, gas 6). Wash and pat dry the bass fillets. Place each fillet on a large square of baking parchment, season and squeeze over a little lemon juice.

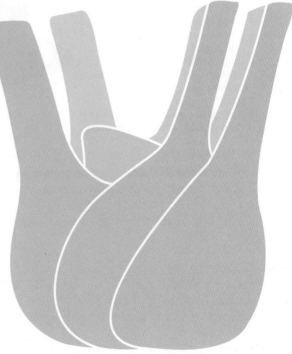

Pile the fennel and herbs on top of each fillet, then drizzle with oil. Bring up the edges of the paper, and fold over each other to seal. Crease to secure. Place the parcels on a baking tray and bake for about 20 minutes until just cooked through.

Serve immediately, straight from the paper, scattered with fresh herbs.

Grilled sardines on toast with fresh tomato salsa

Choose sardines or pilchards for this recipe but make sure they are very fresh. Look for bright eyes and shimmering silvery skin. They are cheap and tasty and can be easily transformed in to a far from humble meal.

Serves 4

12 whole sardines or pilchards, cleaned
Salt and freshly ground black pepper
Juice of 1 lemon
1 tbsp cold pressed rapeseed oil
2 garlic cloves, peeled and finely chopped
4 thick slices country-style white bread, toasted
2 tbsp freshly chopped parsley

For the salsa:
4 large ripe tomatoes
4 spring onions, trimmed and chopped
4 tbsp Smoky red tomato jam (see page 167) or tomato chutney
1 tbsp lemon juice
1 tbsp cold pressed rapeseed oil
2 tbsp freshly chopped parsley

Wash and pat dry the fish. Season the cavities. Lightly slash the flesh of each sardine using a sharp knife and place in a shallow dish. Mix the lemon juice, oil and garlic together and pour over the fish. Cover and chill for 2 hours.

Meanwhile, make the salsa. Mix all the ingredients together, cover and chill until required.

To cook the fish, either arrange in a fish basket and cook over hot barbecue coals for about 5 minutes on each side. Alternatively, preheat the grill to a hot setting. Line the grill pan with foil and arrange the sardines in the pan. Cook for about 5 minutes on each side until cooked through.

To serve, pile three sardines on each piece toasted bread, allowing the cooking juices to soak into the bread. Top with a dollop of salsa and sprinkle with chopped parsley. Serve warm for the best flavours.

Home smoked trout with rosemary

There are several ways you can smoke food at home, but the easiest way is Chinese-style, using a covered heavy-based wok. During the smoking process, the temperature is raised to a high enough level to cook the food.

Makes 2

2 medium sized whole trout, cleaned
Salt
Barbecue or home smoking wood chips, such as oak, beech or fruit wood,
A few sprigs fresh rosemary

Wash and pat dry the trout thoroughly. Put in a shallow dish and sprinkle thickly with salt. Cover and chill for 3 hours. Rinse and dry thoroughly.

Measure out sufficient wood chips to cover the base of your wok to a depth of about 2.5 cm (1 in), and then soak the wood chips for 30 minutes in cold water. Drain off the excess water.

Put the fish on a small rack that will fit inside your wok, and push a sprigs of rosemary inside the cavity of each.

Sprinkle the wood chips over the bottom of the wok and add a few sprigs rosemary. Place the wok over a high heat for about 2 minutes until the chips begin to smoulder then reduce the heat and carefully lower the fish rack over the chips. Cover with a layer of foil and a tight fitting lid. Cook over a low/medium heat for about 35 minutes, turning the fish after 20 minutes, but not before, until cooked through – don't have the heat too high as the chips may dry out and catch fire. The fish will flake easily when it is ready. Remove the fish from the wok and serve hot or cold. Smoked fish will keep in the fridge, covered, for about 2 days.

Bacon wrapped monkfish brochettes

Monkfish is probably the most meaty of fishes, with a texture slightly more chewy than other white fish. It is sweetly juicy, but is prone to drying out. Wrapping bacon or Parma ham around chunks of the fish helps prevent this and make sure all the flavour is sealed in.

Serves 4

1 large red pepper
1 large courgette
500 g (1 lb 2 oz) monkfish fillets, skinned
salt and freshly ground black pepper
2 tsp coriander seeds, lightly crushed
10 rashers rindless smoked back bacon
2 tbsp cold pressed rapeseed oil

Halve, deseed and cut the pepper into bite-sized pieces. Trim the courgette, and slice into 1 cm (½ in) thick pieces. Cut the slices in half. Bring a saucepan of water to the boil and blanch the vegetables for 1 minutes. Drain and rinse in cold water to cool.

Wash and pat dry the fish. Cut into pieces about 2 cm (¾ in) thick. Season with salt, pepper and crushed coriander seeds. Set aside.

Slice each rasher of bacon into lengthwise thin strips approx. 1 cm (½ in) thick, then cut each strip in half.

Wrap a strip of bacon around each piece of fish and thread on to kebab skewers along with pieces of pepper and courgette – you should have enough for 8 skewers.

Preheat the grill to a medium/hot setting. Arrange the skewers on the grill rack, brush with oil and cook for 6–7 minutes on each side, until cooked through and golden – on a hot barbecue, they will take 3–4 minutes on each side. Drain on kitchen paper. Serve 2 skewers per person, on a bed of green salad, accompanied with lemon wedges to squeeze over.

Fresh tuna with fresh bean salad

This is my version of the classic tuna and cannelini bean salad, 'tonno e flagio'. Use fresh tuna or shark steak when it's in season, and any fresh bean combination, but runner beans are one of the most delicious for this dish.

Serves 4

675 g (1½ lb) runner beans, topped, tailed and thinly sliced on the diagonal
Salt and freshly ground black pepper
1 small red onion, peeled and thinly sliced
2 tbsp white wine vinegar
2 tsp clear honey
2 tsp wholegrain mustard
2 tbsp freshly chopped dill
4 tbsp cold pressed rapeseed oil
4 x 175 g (6 oz) tuna or shark steaks
225 g (8 oz) cherry tomatoes, halved
A handful of wild rocket

Bring a saucepan of lightly salted water to the boil and cook the beans together, covered, for about 5 minutes until just cooked. Drain well and rinse in cold running water to cool. Drain again and pat dry with kitchen paper.

Turn the beans into a bowl and mix in the onion. Mix the vinegar, honey, mustard, dill and seasoning with 2 tbsp oil, and toss into the vegetables. Cover and chill for 30 minutes.

For the tuna, wash and pat dry the steaks. Brush with remaining oil and season. Heat a griddle pan until very hot and then press the steaks in to the pan 2 minutes. Turn over the press on the other side. Cook for 2 minutes, then reduce the heat to a medium and continue to cook for about 5 minutes, depending on thickness, or until cooked to your liking. Drain and keep warm.

To serve, pile the bean salad on to serving plates and scatter with cherry tomatoes and wild rocket. Top with a piece of tuna. Serve with wedges of lemon to squeeze over.

Potted shrimps

Sweet brown shrimps require only simple seasoning;
they are tender and juicy and a real symbol of the
Summer. You can make this dish with other prawns,
flaked crab or lobster meat as well.

Serves 4

115 g (4 oz) butter
300 g (10 oz) shelled brown shrimps
Pinch of ground nutmeg
Pinch of ground mace
Pinch of cayenne pepper
Freshly ground black pepper

Melt the butter gently in a saucepan. Transfer to a small heatproof dish and
pour in the butter. Allow to cool then chill and leave it to set. Remove the
clarified butter layer from the top and discard the runny liquid underneath.

Melt one third of the clarified butter in a saucepan and stir in the shrimps,
spices and seasoning. Divide between four small ramekins. Chill until set.

Melt the remaining butter and spoon over the tops of the ramekins to seal. Chill
until set. Serve with toasted bread.

Globe artichokes with hot mayonnaise

This magnificent vegetable takes a bit of preparing, but it is always impressive and needs only a simple accompaniment like this one – which is also good with asparagus. Remember to put finger bowls on the table as eating it can be a messy business.

Serves 4

4 globe artichokes
Juice of 2 lemons

For the hot mayonnaise:
6 medium free range egg yolks
175 g (6 oz) unsalted butter, cut into small
    pieces
2 tbsp fresh chicken or vegetable stock (see
    page 156)
Salt and freshly ground black pepper
Pinch of ground nutmeg
2 tsp white wine tarragon vinegar

Trim the stalk level with the base of the head and cut off any damaged outer scales. Slice off the top of the head and trim the points off each scale with scissors. Wash well and stand upside-down to drain. Brush all cut areas of flesh with lemon juice. Pull the central scales apart and scrape out the hairy choke using a teaspoon – I find a grapefruit spoon useful for this.

Bring a large saucepan of water to the boil and add 1 tsp salt and 2 tbsp lemon juice, add the artichokes and boil, uncovered, for 30–40 minutes, depending on size, until tender – they are cooked when a scale can be pulled away easily. Drain well, upside down.

Meanwhile make the hot mayonnaise. Put the egg yolks in a saucepan with 50 g (2 oz) butter, the stock, seasoning and nutmeg. Stir over a very low heat and, as it begins to thicken, gradually add the remaining butter, stirring well between each addition – do not boil otherwise the eggs will scramble. Just before serving, stir in the vinegar and season if necessary. Serve with hot or cold globe artichokes.

Mixed bean and bacon picnic loaf

This is the season for eating outdoors and packing up a delicious picnic to sustain a ravenous appetite – why is it that you feel hungrier al fresco? This picnic loaf makes a change from sandwiches, and you can pack more filling into it to boot!

Cuts into 6 portions

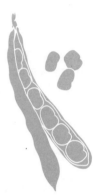

250 g (9 oz) smoked streaky bacon, finely chopped
1 x approx. 20 cm (8 in) round country-style crusty white loaf
200 g (7 oz) cold cooked green beans, cut into short lengths
200 g (7 oz) cold cooked broad beans
1 small green pepper, deseeded and finely chopped
4 spring onions, trimmed and white and green parts finely chopped
2 tbsp cold pressed rapeseed oil
2 tbsp balsamic vinegar
2 tsp locally produced clear honey
Salt and freshly ground black pepper
A small bunch fresh basil

Heat a frying pan and dry fry the bacon for about 5 minutes until just cooked but not crispy. Drain and set aside to cool.

Cut the loaf across, about 2.5 cm (1 in) down from the top. Scoop out the inside crumbs leaving the crust to form a case – the top will be the lid (the crumbs can be used in stuffings and toppings).

In a bowl, mix together the beans, pepper and spring onions. Whisk together the oil, vinegar, sugar and plenty of seasoning and toss into the vegetables. Cover and chill until ready to assemble.

When you are ready, mix the bacon into the vegetables. Pack half the mixture into the loaf and top with a few leaves of basil, then pile the remaining salad on top, and finish with a few more basil leaves. Put the bread lid on top, wrap up tightly in clear wrap and foil and chill for at least an hour. Carefully cut into 6 wedges. Wrap in waxed paper and then brown paper. Tie with string and you're ready to go on your picnic!

Cheesy crumb stuffed courgettes and marrow

Home grown courgettes and marrow have a much sweeter taste than other varieties. Giving them a boost with a tasty stuffing, can make a delicious vegetarian meal out of them, or a filling accompaniment.

Serves 6

50 g (2 oz) butter
4 tbsp cold pressed rapeseed oil
2 garlic cloves, peeled and crushed
1 bunch spring onions, trimmed and chopped
175 g (6 oz) wholemeal breadcrumbs
50 g (2 oz) toasted pine nuts, crushed
50 g (2 oz) shelled unsalted pistachio nuts, crushed
2 tbsp freshly chopped sage
75 g (3 oz) grated local Cheddar-type cheese
4 medium courgettes, washed
1 small marrow, washed

Preheat the oven to 200°C (400°F, gas 6). Melt the butter with the oil in a frying pan until bubbling, then gently fry the garlic and spring onions for 2 minutes until softened but not browned. Set aside to cool for 10 minutes.

Put the breadcrumbs in a heatproof bowl and stir in the nuts, sage and cheese. Season well and set aside. Scoop out the centre of each courgette. Slice the marrow into eight rounds and scoop out the seeds.

Mix the buttery onion mixture into the crumbs and bind together to form a stuffing. Pack the stuffing into the courgettes and marrow slices and arrange in a single layer in a large shallow baking dish. Pour in sufficient water to just cover the base of the dish. Cover the dish with foil and bake for 30 minutes. Remove the foil and cook for a further 20 minutes or until tender and lightly golden. Serve immediately.

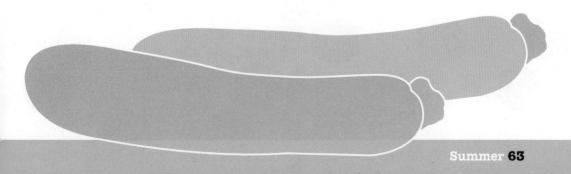

Barbecued lettuce salad

Probably not the first thing you'd think of to put on the barbecue, but a hot salad is a lovely accompaniment to other barbecued food. Choose firm-centred or close-leaved lettuce for best results.

Serves 4

4 tbsp walnut or other nut oil
2 tbsp white wine vinegar
1 tsp clear honey
1 tsp wholegrain mustard
Salt and freshly ground black pepper
2 little gem lettuce
1 head radicchio
25 g (1 oz) toasted chopped walnuts or other nuts

First make the dressing. Place the oil, vinegar, honey, mustard and seasoning in a small screw-top jar and shake well to mix. Set aside.

Discard the outer leaves from the lettuces. Halve the little gems, and quarter the radicchio. Brush with a little of the dressing.

Place over hot coals and cook for about 2 minutes until lightly browned and slightly wilted. Serve warm, drizzled with the remaining dressing and scattered with the chopped nuts.

Fire-cooked potato and corn skewers

Entertaining outdoors is probably one of the nicest pleasures of long summer days, and a barbecue is always a popular social event. Cook these sizzling vegetable kebabs alongside your other goodies – they can be prepared in advance and only take minimal cooking.

Makes 8 skewers

16 same size baby potatoes, scrubbed
Salt and freshly ground black pepper
3 cobs sweet corn
1 tsp caster sugar
4 spring onions, trimmed and cut into 4 equal-sized batons
2 tbsp Worcestershire sauce
2 tbsp sunflower oil

Put the potatoes in a small saucepan and cover with water. Add a pinch of salt and bring to the boil. Cook for 8–10 minutes until just tender. Drain well and set aside to cool.

Meanwhile, strip away the leaves and strings from the sweet corn. Using a large heavy knife, carefully cut each cob into 4 equal slices. Bring a saucepan of water to the boil, add the sugar and sweet corn and blanch for 2 minutes. Drain well and set aside to cool.

Thread 2 potatoes, 2 pieces corn and 2 pieces spring onion alternately on to 8 skewers. Cover and chill until ready to cook.

To cook, mix the Worcestershire sauce and oil together and brush over the vegetables. Cook over hot coals for 5–7 minutes, turning and basting frequently, until lightly charred and tender. Serve hot.

Tían of Provençale vegetables

A colourful masterpiece of a dish – arranged summer vegetables look stunning baked in rows like this, and they taste delicious and meltingly tender. Makes a luscious light supper, or an excellent accompaniment to fish and poultry dishes.

Serves 4

1 large aubergine
3 garlic cloves, peeled and crushed
120 ml (4 fl oz) cold pressed rapeseed oil
4 tbsp freshly chopped parsley
Freshly ground black pepper
2 medium courgettes, trimmed and sliced on the diagonal
4 ripe tomatoes, sliced
1 large yellow pepper, deseeded and cut into thick lengthways strips
A few sprigs fresh thyme
A few sprigs fresh rosemary
A few leaves of fresh basil

Trim the aubergine and cut into thin slices. Layer in a colander or large sieve sprinkling with salt as you go and set aside to drain for 30 minutes. Rinse well in cold water, then pat dry with kitchen paper. Preheat the oven to 200°C (400°F, gas 6).

Mix the garlic, oil and parsley together, and brush a little over each slice of aubergine. Arrange alternate lines of vegetables in a shallow baking dish, , seasoning with black pepper as you go, repeating the sequence to fill the dish. Put the dish on a baking sheet.

Drizzle the vegetables evenly with the garlic oil and lay springs of thyme and rosemary on top. Bake in the oven for about 40 minutes until lightly golden and tender. Stand for at least 10–20 minutes to allow the flavours to develop before serving. Discard the thyme and rosemary and scatter with fresh basil. Best served warm or at room temperature for maximum flavour. Accompany with crusty bread.

Salad of strawberries, smoked salmon and cucumber

Unlike most other berries, strawberries are seldom used in savoury dishes, but they blend very well with other mild flavours. Choose the sweetest you can find and you'll discover just how good they can be pepped up with black pepper and a little balsamic or fruit vinegar.

Serves 4

1 medium cucumber
300 g (10 oz) small strawberries
350 g (12 oz) lightly smoked salmon
A handful of lamb's lettuce
A handful of wild rocket
2 tbsp white balsamic or fruit vinegar
Freshly ground black pepper

Peel the cucumber and slice very thinly. Place in a mixing bowl. Wash and hull the strawberries. Halve and add to the bowl. Gently mix together. Set aside. Slice the smoked salmon into ribbon-like strips and set aside.

Mix the salad leaves together and pile on to serving plates. Top with the cucumber and strawberries and some smoked salmon. Drizzle with vinegar and a generous grind of black pepper. Best served at room temperature, accompanied with a crisp chilled rosé wine or pink champagne!

Blueberry Arctic roll

This famous readymade
70s dessert of frozen
sponge, jam and vanilla
ice cream was the height
of sophistication for me as
a child. This is my version
for grown ups!

Serves 8

450 g (1 lb) good quality vanilla ice cream
150 g (5 oz) blueberries

For the sponge:
3 free range eggs
75 g (3 oz) caster sugar
50 g (2 oz) plain flour
1 tbsp cornflour
1 tbsp hot water
2 tbsp cocoa powder
6 tbsp blueberry jam (see page 159)

Take the ice cream out of the freezer
and allow to soften slightly, then
transfer to a bowl. Wash and pat dry
the blueberries, and carefully mix into
the ice cream. Pile onto a large double-
thickness sheet of baking parchment
and bring up the parchment to form
a tube. Gently squeeze to form a tube
about 19 cm (7 in) long. Wrap in foil
and place in the freezer for at least
2 hours to firm up.

Meanwhile, make the sponge. Preheat
the oven to 220°C (425°F, gas 7).
Grease a 33 x 23 cm (13 x 9 in)
Swiss roll tin. Cut a piece of baking
parchment about 5 cm (2 in) larger
all round than the tin. Press the
parchment into the tin, creasing to
fit sides. Cut the parchment at the

corners of the tin and overlap the cut
paper to fit snugly.

Put the eggs and sugar in a large
clean bowl and whisk until thick, pale
and creamy – this will take about
5 minutes.

Sift the flour, cornflour and cocoa on
to a sheet of greaseproof paper and
then sift into the bowl. Carefully fold
in the dry ingredients along with the
hot water.

Pour the mixture into the prepared
tin and spread the mixture in an
even layer. Bake in the oven for
7–9 minutes until well risen and just
firm to the touch.

Meanwhile, place a sheet of baking
parchment over a clean, damp tea
towel. Working quickly, turn out the
cooked sponge on to the paper, peel
away the lining paper, and cut off the
sponge crusts. Cover with another
sheet of baking parchment and
another damp tea towel. Allow to cool.

To assemble, uncover the sponge and
spread evenly with jam. Carefully
unwrap the ice cream and lay along
one short end of the sponge. Roll up
tightly using the parchment to help.
Wrap the parchment round the sponge
and freeze for a further 30 minutes.
To serve, unwrap the Arctic roll, trim
away any excess sponge. Using a large
sharp knife, cut the roll into slices.
Serve immediately with pouring cream
and extra blueberries if liked.

Fresh peach melba

There's nothing like a fresh ripe peach served at room temperature so that its flowery fragrance can be enjoyed and it's juices drip down your chin as you bite into it. Traditionally, peaches are poached for this recipe, but I make a quicker version which is great as a last minute summery pudding.

Serves 4

4 ripe peaches
4 tsp orange flower water
200 g (7 oz) fresh raspberries
2 tbsp icing sugar
150 ml (5 fl oz) whipping cream
½ tsp vanilla extract
4 generous scoops of raspberry sorbet
4 generous scoops of good quality vanilla
   ice cream

Wash and pat dry the peaches. Halve and remove the stones, and cut in to thick slices. Put in a shallow dish and sprinkle with the orange flower water. Cover and set aside in a cool place for 30 minutes – if serving soon, try to avoid putting in the fridge unless it is very hot.

Wash and pat dry the raspberries. Press through a nylon sieve over a small bowl to remove the seeds and purée the fruit. Sieve in the icing sugar and carefully whisk in. Cover and chill until required.

When ready to serve, whip the cream with the vanilla essence until just peaking. Pile the sorbet and ice cream into serving dishes and top with peach slices. Top with a good dollop of vanilla cream. Stir the raspberry sauce and drizzle over the cream to serve.

Soft fruit terrine

I've made many versions of this dessert over the years, and the best thing about it is that you can use whichever combination of soft fruits you prefer, and the same applies to the jelly you choose to use.

Serves 6

135 g (4½ oz) packet raspberry flavour tablet jelly
Approx. 300 ml (10 fl oz) boiling water
300 ml (10 fl oz) dry rosé wine, chilled
1 tbsp rosewater
550 g (1 lb 4 oz) assorted soft fruits such as small strawberries, alpine strawberries, blackberries, raspberries, blueberries, black- and redcurrants, small dessert gooseberries, washed and prepared
Rose-scented geranium leaves to decorate

Put a 900 g (2 lb) loaf tin in the freezer to chill. Meanwhile, break the jelly into cubes and place in a heatproof measuring jug. Pour over sufficient boiling water to the 300 ml (10 fl oz) level. Stir until dissolved and set aside to cool. Stir in the wine and rose water.

Pour a thin layer of the jelly into the bottom of the loaf tin and chill in the fridge for a few minutes until set. Carefully pack half the fruit into the tin – either randomly or in layers – and pour over sufficient jelly to just cover the fruit. Chill for about 1 hour until firm. Spoon over or layer in the remaining fruit and pour over the remaining jelly. Chill for at least 2 hours until completely set.

To serve, fill a large bowl with hot water and dip the tin in the water for a few seconds to loosen. Invert on to a serving plate and gently shake the jelly to release it from the tin. Decorate with leaves and serve with pouring cream.

Chocolate cherry roulade

This dessert is ideal for anyone who can't tolerate wheat. The sponge, rich and dense in taste and light and airy in texture, is the perfect casing for lush, juicy cherries. Chocolate also works well with fresh raspberries or blueberries.

Serves 6

6 large free range eggs, separated
150 g (5 oz) caster sugar
50 g (2 oz) cocoa powder
4 tbsp cherry jam
150 ml (5 fl oz) whipping cream
225 g (8 oz) fresh cherries, stoned and halved
Cocoa powder for dusting

Preheat the oven to 180°C (350°F, gas 4). Grease a 33 x 23 cm (13 x 9 in) Swiss roll tin. Cut a piece of baking parchment about 5 cm (2 in) larger all round than the tin. Press the parchment into the tin, creasing to fit sides. Cut the parchment at the corners of the tin and overlap the cut paper to fit snugly.

In a large bowl, whisk the egg yolks and sugar until very thick and pale. Sieve in the cocoa powder, and using a large metal spoon, fold the ingredients into each other.

In another bowl, whisk the whites until just stiff but not dry and fold these into the mixture. Pour into the prepared tin and smooth the surface. Bake in the middle of the oven for 20 minutes until springy to the touch. Take care not to overcook. Leave to cool in the tin – it will sink on cooling!

When the sponge is cool, turn on to a large sheet of baking parchment and peel away the lining paper. Spread the jam evenly over the surface. Whip the cream until just peaking and spread carefully over the top. Sprinkle the cherries evenly over the cream.

Take hold of one end of the parchment, lift and gently roll the roulade over like a thick Swiss roll, pulling the paper away. The roulade may crack. Put on a serving plate, cover and chill for 30 minutes. Dust with cocoa to serve. Lovely with a soft fruit coulis (see page 171) and pouring cream.

Greengage and almond ricotta cream trifle

I'll admit to not having much culinary experience with greengages until recently. Greengage is the English name for a group of fine tasting plums which are usually green. They are indeed delicious and flavoursome, and are now a firm favourite of mine.

Serves 6

675 g (1½ lb) greengages, halved and stones removed
75 g (3 oz) granulated sugar
115 g (4 oz) amaretti biscuits, lightly crushed
4 tbsp brandy
2 x 250 g (9 oz) tubs ricotta cheese
4 tbsp icing sugar
1 tsp almond extract
150 ml (5 fl oz) whipping cream
25 g (1 oz) toasted flaked almonds

Put the greengages in a saucepan with the granulated sugar and heat gently until the steam rises, Cover and cook gently for 6–8 minutes, stirring occasionally to prevent sticking, until soft and collapsed. Set aside to cool then press through a nylon sieve over a small bowl to purée the fruit.

Meanwhile, put the crushed amarettis in the bottom of a trifle bowl and spoon over the brandy. Stand for about an hour, stirring occasionally, until the brandy is absorbed.

Beat the ricotta cheese in a mixing bowl to soften it and sieve over the icing sugar. Stir in along with the almond essence. Whip the cream until just peaking and fold into the soft cheese. Cover and chill until required.

Spoon the cold greengage purée over the amarettis and top with the ricotta mixture. Cover and chill for an hour before serving sprinkled with the flaked almonds.

Blackcurrant ice cream

If you've got an ice cream maker then you can churn out sorbets and ices to your heart's content, and capture all the flavours of Summer's harvest for later months. If you haven't got the machine to do the work for you, this is a straightforward method for making a deliciously creamy fruity ice cream.

Serves 6

175 g (6 oz) caster sugar
300 ml (10 fl oz) water
450 g (1 lb) fresh blackcurrants
Juice of 1 lime
350 ml (12 fl oz) whipping cream

Put the sugar and water in a saucepan and heat, stirring, until the sugar dissolves. Bring to the boil and add the blackcurrants, simmer gently for 6–8 minutes until soft and syrupy. Stir in the lime juice, and allow to cool.

Press the cold blackcurrants through a nylon sieve, placed over a small bowl to make a purée. Whip the cream until just peaking and fold into the purèe. Transfer to a freezer container and freeze for about 1½ hours until slushy. Beat the mixture to break up the ice crystals and return to the freezer. Beat the mixture twice more at hourly intervals, then cover, seal and freeze for about 2 hours before serving. Stand at room temperature for 15–20 minutes before scooping.

Wild strawberry
Viennese shortcakes

I have hundreds of little strawberry plants running all over my garden, and whilst it's time-consuming to pick them, I adore their floral sweet flavour. If you haven't got a home-grown supply, try this recipe with blueberries, redcurrants or chopped strawberries.

Makes 6

115 g (4 oz) butter, softened
50 g (2 oz) + 1 tbsp icing sugar
115 g (4 oz) plain flour
25 g (1 oz) ground almonds
A few drops vanilla extract
150 g (5 oz) mascarpone cheese
25 g (1 oz) wild or alpine strawberries,
   washed and dried
4 tbsp strawberry jam, sieved

Preheat the oven to 180°C (350°F, gas 4). Put the butter in a mixing bowl and sieve over 50 g (2 oz) icing sugar. Beat until pale and creamy. Sieve in the flour and add the ground almonds and vanilla extract. Mix together to form a firm dough.

Put the dough in a large piping bag fitted with a 1 cm (½ in) star nozzle. Pipe 6 large stars on each of 2 large sheets lined with baking parchment – the cookies will spread and flatten on baking. Bake for about 15 minutes until firm. Cool on the trays for 15 minutes then transfer to a wire rack to cool completely.

To serve, thickly spread mascarpone over the unpiped side of 6 shortcakes and sprinkle over a few strawberries and push them lightly into the soft cheese. On the remaining shortcakes, spread the unpiped side with jam and sandwich together over the strawberries. Serve immediately dusted with remaining icing sugar.

Glazed berry custard tarts

These tarts look so irresistible and they taste divine. They're a lovely way to enjoy small berries at their best.

Makes 10

300 g (10 oz) readymade sweet
   shortcrust pastry or see recipe below
2 medium free range egg yolks
25 g (1 oz) caster sugar
1 tbsp plain flour
1 tbsp cornflour
150 ml (5 fl oz) whole milk
Few drops of vanilla extract
250 g (9 oz) assorted small berries such
   as wild strawberries, raspberries,
   blueberries and blackberries, washed
   and prepared
4 tbsp soft fruit jam such as blueberry,
   strawberry or raspberry, sieved and
   mixed with 1 tbsp cold water

Preheat the oven to 200°C (400°F, gas 6). On a lightly floured surface, roll out the pastry thinly and stamp out 10 rounds using 10 cm (4 in) pastry cutter, re-rolling as necessary. Use to line greased 10 deep cup muffin tins. Chill for 30 minutes.

Meanwhile, make the custard. Whisk the egg yolks and sugar together until pale and thick. Whisk in the flour, cornflour and 2 Tbsp milk to make a smooth paste. Heat the remaining milk until just below boiling point and then pour over the egg and flour paste, whisking until smooth and well combined. Transfer to a small saucepan and stir over a low heat until it comes to the boil and then cook for a further 2 minutes until thick. Remove from the heat, add a few drops of vanilla, cover the surface with a sheet of buttered greaseproof paper and leave aside to cool completely.

Prick the pastry bases all over with a fork, arrange on a baking sheet and bake in the oven for about 15 minutes until lightly golden and firm. Allow to cool before removing from the tins.

When ready to serve, spoon the custard into the pastry cases, leaving a small rim of pastry above the layer of custard. Arrange a few berries on top of each. Carefully spoon or brush over the prepared jam to coat the fruit and flood the top of the custard. Serve within 30 minutes of assembling – the pastry may go soggy after this time.

Tip: To make your own sweet pastry for this recipe: put 200 g (7 oz) plain flour in a food processor with a pinch of salt. Add 100 g (3½ oz) softened butter and blend for a few seconds until well combined. Add 1 tablespoon cold water and process until the mixture comes together. Knead gently on a lightly floured surface until smooth, then wrap and chill for 30 minutes before using.

As a child I can remember going back to school at the beginning of September dressed in our Winter uniforms, only to be faced with some of the most glorious sunny weather we'd seen all Summer. I cling to these thoughts, when September dawns, because this isn't a time of year I relish. Although I love the colours of Autumn, the climate of damp, chilly weather makes this my least favourite time of year.

AUTUMN

(beginning of September, through
October, to the end of November)

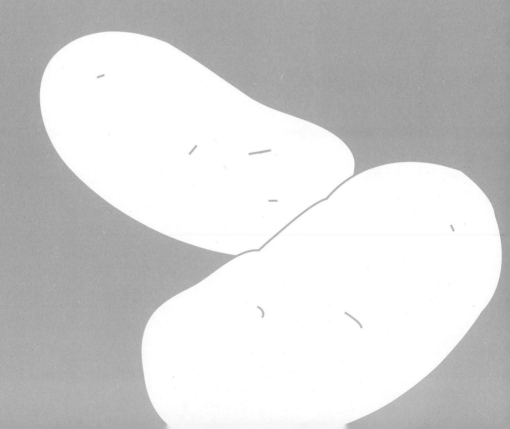

Weather aside, we do have some fabulous foods to look forward to, especially another favourite of mine, hedgerow blackberries, or brambles as they are known in Scotland. Superstition has it that they must be picked before the first frost, as after this time, the devil has rendered them inedible by spitting on them! An unpalatable thought I must say, but actually, it is unlikely you will still find them on the bush much after the middle of September.

To me, autumn produce has a rustic and earthy feel about it. Wild or free foods are in abundance: look out for bright reddish-orange rowan berries which make a rich sweet/sour jelly to serve with meat (just make sure you get them before the birds do!), and the scarlet rose hip from the wild dog rose which is very rich in Vitamin C and makes a delicious cordial – both recipes can be found in the last chapter of the book. On the ground, you might be lucky enough to find wild woodland mushrooms if you know the right places to look, and cooked simply in butter, they will provide you with a wonderful free feast beyond compare. Pumpkin and Winter squash are harvested at this time; their golden orange flesh adds a touch of colour to the dinner plate and their sweet earthy flavoured flesh can be used in sweet and savoury dishes alike, and of course, the shell makes a great 'Jack o lantern' for Hallowe'en.

Game is the real feast of the season, many of us shy away from the feathered and furry creatures we may see hanging in the butcher's windows. I hope I have included a selection of approachable recipes to tempt you into trying out a few of the finest meats (in my opinion) we have to offer in the UK. The fishmonger should be displaying a variety of new season's fish from the aphrodisiac oyster to the finely textured, and extremely ugly, John Dory – don't let its appearance put you off, nothing else matches it for texture.

Apples (Bramley)	new season from October to May
(dessert): George Cave/ Discovery/ Worcester/Pearmain/ Egremont Russet	until October
(dessert): Spartan/Cox's Orange Pippin/Ida Red/ Laxton Superb/Crispin/Golden Delicious	new season from October to March
Beans: runner	until October
kidney	until November
Blackberries (Brambles)	until October
Blueberries	until September
Brussels sprouts	new season from September to March
Cabbages: Summer	until October
Spring greens	new season from November to April
White	new season from October to February
Savoy, Red and Winter	
Celery	
Celeriac	new season from October to March
Chestnuts	new season from October to December
Courgettes	until September
Crab apples (homegrown)	harvest September and October
Damsons	until October
Endive	new season from November to February
Globe artichoke	until September
Horseradish	new season from September to March
Jerusalem artichoke	new season from mid October to March
Kale	new season from September to May
Kohlrabi	
Leeks	
Marrows	until October
Nectarines	until September
Onions: pickling	until December
Parsnips	new season from September to April
Peaches	until October
Pears	
Peas	until October
Peppers	until September
Plums	until October
Potatoes: maincrop	new season from September to March
Pumpkin and squash	until December
Quince	new season from October to November
Raspberries	until September
Salsify	new season from October to May
Shallots	new season from September to March
Strawberries: outdoor	until October
Swede	new season from September to May
Sweetcorn	until November
Tomatoes	until October
Turnips	
Walnuts: green	new season from September and October
Wild mushrooms	until November

MEAT: duck, goose, grouse, guinea fowl, lamb, mutton, partridge, rabbit, venison, wood pigeon
FISH: brill, clams, crab, grey mullet, hake, halibut, John Dory, lemon sole, lobster, mackerel, monkfish, mussels, oysters, plaice, scallops, sea bass, turbot

Mediterranean sweet pepper and squash soup

A bright coloured, sweet tasting earthy soup to help ease you into the new season and the onset of cooler times ahead. If it's an Indian summer, allow the soup to cool, add a little crème fraîche and serve chilled.

Serves 4

1 small butternut or similar squash, cut into 8 pieces and deseeded
2 large red, yellow or orange peppers, deseeded and halved
2 red onions, peeled and quartered
2 large tomatoes, halved
2 garlic cloves, peeled and sliced
A few sprigs fresh rosemary and thyme
Salt and freshly ground black pepper
2 tbsp cold pressed rapeseed oil
1.2 l (40 fl oz) fresh vegetable stock (see page 156)
2 tsp caster sugar
Fresh herbs to garnish

Preheat the oven to 200°C (400°F, gas 6). Arrange the squash, peppers, onions and tomatoes on a large baking sheet lined with baking parchment. Sprinkle over the garlic, herbs and plenty of seasoning. Drizzle with cold pressed rapeseed oil and bake for about 35 minutes or until tender. Discard the herbs.

Scoop out the flesh from the squash and place in a blender or food processor. Add the other roasted vegetables and 300 ml (10 fl oz) stock. Blend for a few seconds until smooth.

Transfer to a large saucepan and stir in the remaining stock. Heat through, stirring, for 4–5 minutes until piping hot. Season with sugar and salt and pepper to taste. Ladle into warmed serving bowls, sprinkle with a few herb leaves and grind over black pepper if liked. Serve immediately.

Note: For a chilled soup, allow the vegetable purée to cool and then mix in the remaining stock and 4 tbsp crème fraîche. Chill for at least an hour before serving over ice cubes.

Wild mushroom soup

Half soup, half creamy mushroom sauté, this is a simple way to enjoy wild mushrooms at their best. This is the time of year when they are in season in the UK, and if you have a wild source near you, then they're one of Nature's finest luxuries. You can replace the wild with any other mushroom of your choosing.

Serves 4

50 g (2 oz) unsalted butter
1 shallot, peeled and finely chopped
1 garlic clove, peeled and finely chopped
500 g (1 lb 2 oz) wild mushrooms, such as chanterelle and cep, cleaned and sliced
120 ml (4 fl oz) dry white wine
150 ml (5 fl oz) double cream
Salt and freshly ground black pepper
Pinch of freshly grated nutmeg
3 tbsp freshly chopped parsley

Melt the butter in a large frying pan until bubbling and gently fry the shallot and garlic for 5 minutes until softened but not browned – take care not to burn the butter by keeping the heat low and steady.

Add the mushrooms and raise the heat. Stir-fry for 1 minute to coat in the butter. Add the wine, and cook covered, for a further minute. Lower the heat and pour in the cream. Season lightly and add nutmeg, and heat through for a few seconds more. Strain the mushrooms, reserving the creamy liquid, into a warm dish and cover and keep warm.

Return the juices to the saucepan and bring to the boil. Cook for 5 minutes until slightly thickened and creamy.

To serve, pile the mushrooms into warmed, shallow soup plates and spoon over the reduced cream. Sprinkle generously with parsley. Serve immediately.

Beef Wellington parcels with damson sauce

Once a statement dish in many restaurants, beef fillet in puff pastry has become a recipe of the past. To my mind, there is no better way to enjoy locally raised beef, so I'm resurrecting it. The tart damson sauce adds a sharp fruity edge.

Serves 4

For the mushrooms:
15 g (½ oz) unsalted butter
½ small onion, peeled and finely chopped
175 g (6 oz) mushrooms of choice, wiped and finely chopped
1 tbsp mushroom ketchup
2 tbsp freshly chopped parsley
Salt and freshly ground black pepper

For the filling:
15 g (½ oz) unsalted butter
1 tbsp cold pressed rapeseed oil
4 x 150 g (5 oz) lean fillet beef steaks, trimmed
100 g (3½ oz) liver paté
500 g (1 lb 2 oz) puff pastry
1 free range egg, beaten, to glaze

For the sauce:
350 g (12 oz) damsons
150 ml (5 fl oz) water
2 tbsp raspberry vinegar
3–4 tbsp caster sugar

First make the mushroom filling. Melt the butter until bubbling, then gently fry the onion for 5 minutes until softened but not browned. Add the mushrooms and cook over a high heat, stirring occasionally, for about 10 minutes until the mushrooms are cooked down and the liquid has evaporated. Remove from the heat and stir in the ketchup. Season lightly and set aside to cool. For the beef, melt the butter with the cold pressed rapeseed oil until bubbling and hot then seal the steaks for 1 minute on each side. Drain and season, and allow to cool.

Meanwhile, make the sauce. Put the damsons in a saucepan with the water. Bring to the boil and simmer gently for 7–8 minutes until soft and pulpy. Cool for 10 minutes, then push through a nylon sieve to make a thick pulp. Allow to cool. Stir in the vinegar and add sufficient sugar to taste. Cover and chill until required.

Preheat the oven to 220°C, (425°F, gas 7). Roll out the pastry on a lightly floured board to a 36-cm (14-in) square and cut into quarters. Divide the mushroom mixture between the centre of each square and top with a slice of paté. Lay a steak on top and brush the pastry with egg. Wrap the pastry over the steaks, folding it to make a neat 'parcel'. Seal the edges together and place seam-side down on a baking tray lined with baking parchment. Lightly slash the tops using a sharp knife. Brush with egg and bake for about 25 minutes until cooked to a medium doneness – for a rarer beef cook for about 20 minutes, and 30 minutes cooking will give you a well done steak.

Serve immediately with the damson sauce and freshly cooked vegetables.

Moroccan spiced lamb shanks with crushed pumpkin

My favourite spices are those frequently used in the Middle Eastern kitchen. Warming and fragrant, they really make you feel good. This is a slow cooked dish that cooks lamb to a melting-tenderness so it literally falls off the bone. The earthy-flavoured accompaniment makes the meal perfectly complete.

Serves 4

Salt and freshly ground black pepper
2 tsp cumin seeds, roasted and lightly crushed
2 tsp coriander seeds, roasted and lightly crushed
4 x 225 g (8 oz) lean lamb shanks, trimmed
2 tbsp cold pressed rapeseed oil
1 large onion, peeled and chopped
2 tbsp plain flour
500 ml (17 fl oz) fresh chicken stock (see page 156)
1 small cinnamon stick, broken
410-g can chickpeas, drained and rinsed
750 g (1 lb 10 oz) pumpkin, deseeded, skinned and chopped
½ tsp finely grated orange rind
2 tbsp freshly squeezed orange juice
1 tbsp light brown sugar
4 tbsp freshly chopped coriander

Preheat the oven to 170°C (325°F, gas 3). Mix some salt and pepper together with the cumin and coriander and then rub into the lamb, all over. Heat the oil in a large frying pan and cook the lamb for about 5 minutes, turning it in the oil, to seal it all over. Transfer to a casserole using a slotted spoon, reserving the cooking juices in the pan.

Reheat the juices and add the onion. Cook, stirring, for 5 minutes until softened then stir in the flour to make a paste. Gradually stir in the stock and bring to the boil, stirring constantly, and simmer for 5 minutes. Pour over the lamb and add the cinnamon stick. Cover with a layer of foil and then the lid. Cook for 2 hours, turning the lamb halfway through, and stirring in the chickpeas. Discard the cinnamon stick.

Fifteen minutes before the end of cooking time, put the pumpkin in a saucepan. Cover with water and add a good pinch of salt. Bring to the boil and cook for 10–12 minutes until tender. Drain well and return to the saucepan. Mash lightly using a fork or potato masher. Stir in the remaining ingredients, except the chopped coriander, season well and keep warm.

To serve, divide the pumpkin mixture between 4 warmed serving plates and sprinkle generously with chopped coriander. Top each with a lamb shank. Spoon over the sauce and serve immediately.

Honey glazed sausages with mustard and onion mash

We Brits make great sausages, and it's always a delight to find a really special one. I think this recipe works best with either a lightly herbed or plain pork sausage, but it's up to you to experiment with your local favourite.

Serves 4

12 chunky pork sausages
2 tbsp clear honey
1 tbsp sunflower oil
1 medium onion, peeled and thinly sliced
Pinch of freshly grated nutmeg

For the mash:
900 g (2 lb) potatoes such as King Edward,
    Maris Piper or Rooster, peeled and chopped
Salt
25 g (1 oz) butter
1 medium onion, peeled and chopped
2 tbsp wholegrain mustard
2 tbsp double cream
Freshly ground black pepper

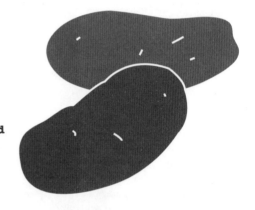

Preheat the oven to 200°C (400°F, gas 6). Arrange the sausages in a small shallow roasting tin on a layer of baking parchment – this will help save the tin if the honey over-caramelises. Mix the honey and oil together and brush thickly over the sausages. Sprinkle with the sliced onion and nutmeg. Bake for about 25 minutes, basting occasionally, until rich brown and cooked through.

Meanwhile, make the mash. Put the potatoes in a saucepan and cover with water. Add a generous pinch of salt, bring to the boil and cook for 10–15 minutes, until tender. Drain well and return to the saucepan. Whilst the potatoes are cooking, melt the butter until bubbling and gently fry the onion for 5 minutes until softened but not brown. Set aside.

Mash the cooked potato well and stir in the buttery onion and remaining ingredients. Mix well, cover and keep warm.

To serve, pile the mash on to 4 warm serving plates and top each with 3 sausages. Serve with green vegetables and extra mustard if liked.

Warm guinea fowl salad with lavender dressing

Even when there's an autumnal nip in the air, you can still enjoy a salad. This one captures some of the flavours of Summer along side some of the season's finest ingredients. Chicken or duck will also work well here.

Serves 4

4 boneless guinea fowl breasts
Salt and freshly ground black pepper
3 tbsp sunflower oil
15 g (½ oz) butter
4 shallots, peeled and sliced
2 tbsp lavender vinegar (see page 150)
2 tsp caster sugar
2 large heads chicory, outer leaves discarded, trimmed
6 ripe figs, quartered

Remove any excess skin from the guinea fowl breasts, and take out the sinew from each piece. Wash and pat dry, then season all over.

Heat 1 tbsp oil with the butter until frothy and bubbling and add the breasts, skin-side down; fry gently for 7–8 minutes, browning slightly. Turn over and continue to cook for a further 7–8 minutes, or until cooked through and golden. Drain reserving the pan juices, and keep warm.

Gently fry the shallots in the reserved pan juices, stirring, for about 5 minutes until softened. Drain and keep warm.

Place the vinegar in a small screw top jar with the remaining oil, sugar and some seasoning. Seal and shake well to mix. Break up the chicory leaves and divide between 4 serving plates. Top each with six fig quarters. Cut each guinea fowl breast into 4 or 5 thick slices and arrange on top of the figs and leaves. Spoon over shallots and drizzle with dressing to serve whilst still warm.

Roast partridge with plum and Madeira sauce

In season from 1st September to 1st February, the early birds up to November are the best to enjoy. The meat is pale in colour and has a fine texture and flavour.

Serves 4

4 small red leg partridges, approx. 250 g (9 oz) each), wings removed
Salt and freshly ground white pepper
8 slices unsmoked streaky bacon
1 tbsp sunflower oil
25 g (1 oz) unsalted butter
450 g (1 lb) plums, quartered
1 tbsp local honey
120 ml (4 fl oz) Madeira
150 ml (5 fl oz) fresh chicken stock (see page 156)

Preheat the oven to 200°C (400°F, gas 6). Wash and pat dry the birds, then season all over and inside. Tie the birds' legs together with string. Cut each slice of bacon in half and arrange 4 pieces overlapping to cover the breasts of each bird.

Put the birds in a roasting tin and bake for about 30 minutes, basting with any juices and making sure that the bacon stays on the birds, until cooked through.

Melt the butter in a saucepan and add the plums and honey. Cook, stirring, for 5 minutes until softening. Pour over the Madeira and stock, bring to the boil and simmer for 5 minutes until tender and pulpy. Push through a nylon sieve to remove the skins and stones.

To serve, discard the bacon and remove the string. Slice off the legs and breasts from the birds, and arrange one of each piece per warmed serving plate. Serve with freshly cooked vegetables and the plum sauce.

Wild duck with quince mash

Although 'wild duck' encompasses several species, it is usually the mallard that is associated with the term. All species are season from 1st September to 31st January. Not fatty like other duck, wild meat becomes tough and flavourless if cooked through – it is best served slightly underdone.

Serves 4

Pared rind and juice 1 lemon
200 ml (7 fl oz) water
1 large quince
2.5 cm (1 in) piece root ginger, peeled and finely sliced
50 g (2 oz) caster sugar
2 wild mallard ducks, approx. 675 g (1½ lb) each, wings removed
Salt and freshly ground white pepper
150 g (5 fl oz) ruby port

Put the lemon rind ad juice in a bowl and pour over the water. Peel and core the quince, and chop into small pieces, adding to the lemony water as quickly as possible to prevent discolouration. Transfer the quince and water to a saucepan and add the ginger and sugar. Bring slowly to the boil, stirring until the sugar dissolves, then simmer, half covered, for 15–20 minutes until very tender. Discard the lemon rind and mash to a pulp using a potato masher. Keep warm.

Meanwhile, preheat the oven to 200°C (400°F, gas 6). Wash and pat dry the ducks and season all over and inside. Using lengths of clean string, tie the bird's legs together.

Put the ducks in a small roasting tin lined with baking parchment, pour over the port and bake for about 40 minutes, basting occasionally, until pink, or until cooked to your liking. Note: the port acts as a steam bath for the birds as they cook; the baking parchment helps keep the tin bottom free from the caramelised port.

To serve, remove the string and slice off the legs and breasts from the birds. Put a dollop of the quince mash on four warmed serving plates and arrange one of each piece of duck on top. Serve with freshly cooked vegetables.

Roast grouse with bread sauce and parsnip game chips

Probably the most well known of all the game birds because of its 'glorious' 12th (August) connotations, grouse has a strong gamey flavour. The birds are at their best until mid October but the season lasts until 10th December.

Serves 4

For the sauce:
300 ml (10 fl oz) whole milk
1 small onion, peeled and studded with 3 cloves
1 bay leaf
Pinch of ground mace or nutmeg
50 g (2 oz) fresh white breadcrumbs
25 g (1 oz) butter
Salt and freshly ground white pepper

For the grouse:
4 young plump grouse, wings removed
8 rashers unsmoked streaky bacon

For the chips:
2 medium parsnips
Sunflower oil for deep-frying

First make the sauce, pour the milk into a saucepan and add the onion, bay leaf and mace or nutmeg. Bring to the boil, cover and simmer very gently for 30 minutes. Allow to cool, then strain into another saucepan. Stir in the breadcrumbs, butter and seasoning. Cook over a low heat, stirring occasionally, for about 15 minutes until thick. Serve hot, adding a little more milk if too thick. Preheat the oven to 190°C (375°F, gas 5).

For the grouse, wash and pat dry and then season lightly all over and inside. Using lengths of clean string, tie the birds' legs together. Cut each slice of bacon in half and arrange 4 pieces overlapping to cover the breasts of each bird.

Place in a roasting tin. Bake in the oven for 40–45 minutes, basting frequently, until cooked through. Drain and rest, covered with foil, for 10 minutes.

Whilst the grouse are resting, peel the parsnips and slice very thinly lengthways. Heat the oil to 190°C (375°F). Pat the parsnip slices as dry as possible using absorbent kitchen paper and then deep fry a few slices at a time for 4–5 minutes until crisp and golden. Drain on kitchen paper and keep warm whilst frying the other slices.

To serve, discard the bacon and remove the string and slice off the legs and breasts from the birds. Arrange on warm serving plates, legs side by side, and then the breasts on top. Accompany with the bread sauce and parsnip chips, and serve with fruit jelly and fresh watercress.

Oyster and scallop stew

Early Autumn is a good time of year for most shellfish, and any can be used to make this creamy rich and flavoursome dish. Traditionally speaking, shellfish is at its prime when there is an 'R' in the month.

Serves 4

50 g (2 oz) unsalted butter
4 rashers smoked streaky bacon, finely chopped
1 large carrot, peeled and finely diced
1 parsnip, peeled and finely diced
4 shallots, peeled and finely diced
2 sticks celery, trimmed and finely diced
2 garlic, cloves, peeled and finely diced
150 ml (5 fl oz) dry white wine
150 ml (5 fl oz) fresh fish stock (see page 156)
200 ml (7 fl oz) double cream
12 oysters, removed from the shell and juices reserved
12 scallops, removed from the shell and juices reserved
Salt and freshly ground black pepper
4 tbsp freshly chopped parsley

Melt the butter in a large saucepan until bubbling and fry the bacon for 4–5 minutes until lightly brown. Add the vegetables and garlic and cook over a low heat, stirring, for about 10 minutes until softened. Add the wine and stock, bring to the boil and cook for 2 minutes. Pour in the cream, bring back to the boil and cook for a further 2 minutes until slightly reduced.

Add the oysters and scallops along with the reserved juices. Bring to a gentle simmer and cook for about 5 minutes, turning occasionally, until just cooked through. Taste and season, then ladle into warmed serving bowls and sprinkle with parsley. Ideal served spooned over freshly cooked rice and accompanied with green vegetables.

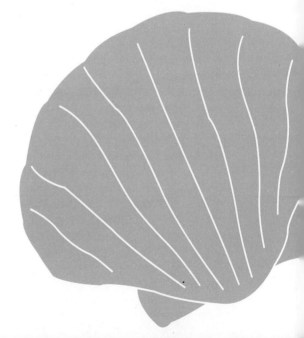

Kedgeree

Traditionally a substantial breakfast dish from the days of the British Empire's rule in India, but now more widely served at supper. There are many recipes but I think the best kedgeree is made simply from smoked haddock, rice with a hint of curry. Top with hard-boiled eggs for added breakfast appeal, if liked.

Serves 4

1 tbsp sunflower oil
25 g (1 oz) unsalted butter
1 large onion, peeled and finely chopped
225 g (8 oz) Basmati rice, rinsed
975 ml (33 fl oz) water
Salt and freshly ground black pepper
6 cardamom pods, cracked
1 bay leaf
2 tsp mild curry powder
¼ tsp cayenne pepper
450 g (1 lb) smoked haddock fillet
3 tbsp freshly chopped coriander

Heat the oil with the butter in a large saucepan until frothy and bubbling and gently fry the onion for 5 minutes until softened but not browned. Add the rice and cook, stirring all the time, for 1 minute until well coated in the buttery onion.

Pour in the water and add seasoning, cardamom, bay leaf, curry powder and the cayenne. Bring to the boil, cover and simmer gently for 12–15 minutes until the rice is tender and the liquid absorbed. Discard the cardamom pods and bay leaf.

Meanwhile, put the haddock in a shallow pan and pour in sufficient water to just cover it. Bring to the boil, then cover and simmer gently for 7–8 minutes until just cooked through. Drain well and flake away from the skin, keeping the haddock in bite-sized pieces. Keep warm.

To assemble the dish, drain the rice if necessary and return it to the saucepan. Gently fold in the flaked haddock and the coriander. Pile on to warm serving plates and accompany with grilled tomatoes.

Smoked fish cakes with beetroot

Unusual looking but tasting fabulous, these beautiful pink fishcakes will certainly be a talking point. Serve with freshly grated horseradish relish to pack a flavour punch (see page 155).

Serves 4

225 g (8 oz) small beetroot
Salt and freshly ground black pepper
225 g (8 oz) firm potatoes, such as Maris Piper, King Edward or Rooster
50 g (2 oz) unsalted butter
2 shallots, peeled and finely chopped
400 g (14 oz) smoked mackerel fillets
4 tbsp freshly chopped parsley
4 tbsp plain flour
2 free range eggs, beaten
115 g (4 oz) fresh white breadcrumbs
150 ml (5 fl oz) sunflower oil, for shallow frying

Trim the beetroot leaving the root intact. Place in a saucepan and cover with lightly salted water. Bring to the boil and cook for about 1½ hours. Drain and rinse under cold running water until cool enough to handle, then carefully rub off the skins. Allow to cool completely, and then grate coarsely into a bowl.

Meanwhile, peel and dice the potato. Place in a saucepan with a pinch of salt and cover with water. Bring to the boil and cook for 10–12 minutes until tender. Drain well, return to the saucepan and mash until smooth. Set aside to cool.

Melt the butter in a frying pan until bubbling and fry the shallot for 5 minutes until softened but not brown. Stir into the mashed potato and allow to cool.

Flake the mackerel away from the skins and mix into the mashed potato along with the grated beetroot. Season well and stir in the parsley.

Sieve the flour on to a plate; put the egg on to another, and the breadcrumbs on another. Divide the fish mixture into 8 and form each into a ball, using a little flour to dust your fingers. Flatten into 'cakes' and dust in flour, then dip in egg, then coat in crumbs. Place on a board lined with baking parchment, cover and chill for 1 hour.

Heat the oil for shallow frying in a large frying pan until hot then gently fry the fish cakes for 4–5 minutes on each side until crisp and golden. Drain well and serve with horseradish relish

John Dory with garlic potatoes

This quite ugly looking fish is caught off English shores all the way down to Morocco, and it is at its best in the UK in late Autumn and Winter. You'll probably be disappointed when you see the size of the fish against the yield you're likely to get from it, but the flesh is moist and tender, and can be enjoyed in many ways.

Serves 4

675 g (1½ lb) potatoes, such as Maris Piper
   or Rooster, peeled and very thinly sliced
75 g (3 oz) unsalted butter, melted
1 garlic clove, peeled and crushed
150 ml (5 fl oz) dry white wine
Salt and freshly ground black pepper
A pinch ground nutmeg
2 x 675g (1½ lb) John Dory, cleaned, fins
   removed
6 tbsp freshly chopped parsley

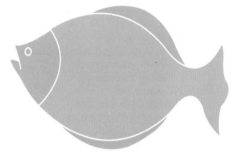

Preheat the oven to 190°C (375°F, gas 5). Bring a saucepan of water to the boil and add the potato slices. Bring back to the boil and cook for 3–5 minutes until opaque but not soft. Drain well through a colander or large sieve and air dry for 10 minutes.

Mix the butter and garlic together and brush a large baking dish with a little of the butter. Layer the potato slices evenly in the dish, seasoning with salt, pepper and nutmeg and drizzling with butter as you go, reserving a little butter for the fish. Finally, lay the fish on top and drizzle with reserved butter.

Pour the wine over the dish. Stand the dish on a baking tray, cover with foil and bake in the oven for 20 minutes. Remove the foil, baste well and cook for a further 20 minutes until the potatoes and fish are tender. Serve sprinkled with chopped parsley, and accompany with crusty bread to mop up the juices.

Oyster Po'boy sandwich

Originating from the Southern States of America, and considered to be the cheapest lunch possible – even a 'poor boy' could afford one – they were simply slices of French bread, hollowed out and packed with whatever was the cheapest food of the day, which was often oysters. Today it makes a great hot treat, and can be whipped up in next to no time.

Serves 1

1 chunky piece crusty white bread
6 oysters, removed from their shells
2 tbsp plain flour
Salt and freshly ground black pepper
Pinch cayenne pepper
25 g (1 oz) unsalted butter
Dash Tabasco sauce
Squeeze of lemon juice
1 spring onion, trimmed and finely chopped

Cut the bread in half through the middle and hollow out some of the soft bread from the middle of one piece, making a slight indent for the oyster filling.

Wash and pat dry the oysters. Sieve the flour on to a small plate and season with salt, pepper and cayenne pepper. Toss the oysters in the flour to coat lightly.

Melt the butter in a small frying pan until bubbling and frothy and the stir-fry the oysters for about a minute in the hot butter until just cooked through. Immediately spoon over the indented bread allowing the melted butter and pan juices to soak into the loaf. Add a dash of Tabasco, a little lemon juice and sprinkle with spring onion. Top with the other piece of bread and serve immediately.

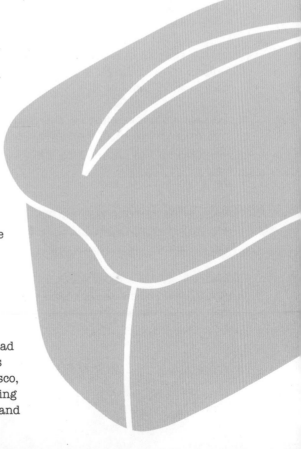

Grilled mackerel with sherry vinegar and shallot relish

This tasty, tangy relish is the perfect partner to oily fish such as mackerel. Shallots are sweet tasting at this time of year and their hint-of-pink coloured flesh makes a pretty addition to any plate.

Serves 4

**225 g (8 oz) shallots, peeled and finely sliced
2 tbsp sherry vinegar
1 tbsp sunflower oil
2 tsp caster sugar
150 ml (5 fl oz) fresh vegetable stock (see page 156)
1 tsp cornflour
8 x 100g (3½ oz) mackerel fillets
Salt and freshly ground black pepper
2 tbsp freshly chopped chives**

Put the shallots in a bowl and toss in 1 tbsp sherry vinegar. Set aside for 5 minutes. Heat the oil in a frying pan and fry the shallots with the soaking vinegar for 5 minutes until tender but not browned. Add the caster sugar and pour over the stock, bring to the boil and simmer for 5 minutes. Mix the remaining vinegar with the cornflour to make a paste and stir into the onion mixture, stirring, until thickened. Cook for a further minute, season and set aside whilst cooking the mackerel.

Wash and pat dry the mackerel fillets and season on both sides.

Preheat the grill to a medium/hot setting. Arrange the mackerel fillets on the grill rack, flesh-side up, and cook for 5–6 minutes, without turning, until tender and cooked through. Drain well.

Spoon the warm shallot relish on to four warmed serving plates and top each with 2 mackerel fillets. Sprinkle with chopped chives and serve accompanied with freshly cooked vegetables.

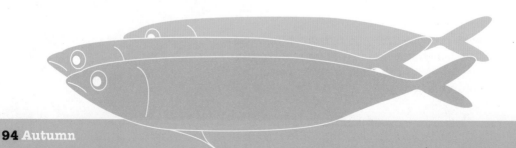

Squash and blue cheese risotto

There's nothing complicated about making a risotto, you just need a bit of time and patience. The earthy flavour of squash goes very well with blue cheese, and the rice cooks to a golden yellow which looks warm and inviting.

Serves 4

1.2 l (40 fl oz) fresh vegetable stock (see page 156)
50 g (2 oz) butter
2 shallots, peeled and finely chopped
1 garlic clove, peeled and finely chopped
450 g (1 lb) prepared squash or pumpkin flesh, cut into small cubes
400 g (14 oz) Arborio rice
Pinch of saffron
150 g (5 oz) local firm blue cheese
Salt and freshly ground black pepper
Grated nutmeg to dust

Pour the stock into a saucepan and bring to the boil. Reduce the heat to a gentle simmer.

Meanwhile, melt the butter in a large saucepan and gently fry the shallots and garlic for 5 minutes until softened but not browned. Add the squash or pumpkin and cook, stirring, for 6–7 minutes until just beginning to soften. Add the rice and saffron and cook, stirring, for 2 minutes, until well mixed.

Add a ladleful of stock and cook gently, stirring, until absorbed. Continue adding the stock ladle by ladle to the rice until half the stock is used and the rice is creamy.

Add the remaining stock until the risotto becomes thick, but not sticky. This will take about 25 minutes and should not be hurried. Just before serving, crumble or cut the cheese into small chunks, then carefully fold into the rice. Taste and season and serve immediately sprinkled with nutmeg.

Mushroom and buckwheat crepe bake

The flavours of this dish are earthy and woody. Use any variety of mushrooms for the filling.

Serves 6

For the crepes:
40 g (1½ oz) buckwheat flour
25 g (1 oz) plain flour
Pinch of salt
1 free range egg
1 free range egg yolk
150 ml (5 fl oz) whole milk
65 g (2½ oz) unsalted butter, melted

For the filling:
900 g (2 lb) selection mushrooms, cleaned and wiped
50 g (2 oz) unsalted butter
1 onion, peeled and finely chopped
1 garlic clove, peeled and finely chopped
Few sprigs fresh thyme
2 tbsp mushroom ketchup
Salt and freshly ground black pepper

For the sauce:
4 tbsp cornflour
600 ml (20 fl oz) whole milk
100 g (3½ oz) mild firm cheese, grated

First make the crepes. Combine the flours and salt in a bowl and make a well in the centre. Add the egg and yolk and half the milk. Gradually work into the flour using a whisk. Beat lightly until smooth, then gently whisk in the remaining milk. Transfer to a jug, cover and stand for 30 minutes. Stir in 50 g (2 oz) melted butter just before using.

Lightly brush a small frying pan with a little butter and heat until hot. Pour in 50 ml (2 fl oz) batter and tilt the pan to form a thin, even layer. Cook over a moderate heat for 1–2 minutes until lightly brown, turn over and cook for a further minute. Turn on to a wire rack and top with a sheet of baking parchment. Repeat to make another 5 crepes.

For the filling, slice the mushrooms into small, even pieces. Melt the butter in a large saucepan and gently fry the onion and garlic for 5 minutes until softened. Add the mushrooms and ketchup, stir well, bring to the boil, add a few sprigs of thyme, and cook, stirring occasionally, for about 20 minutes until reduced. Cool, season and discard the thyme.

Meanwhile, make the sauce. Blend the cornflour with a little of the milk to make a paste. Pour the remaining milk into a saucepan and add the cornflour paste. Bring to the boil, stirring, and cook for 1 minute until thick. Drain the mushrooms well, reserving the cooking liquid, and add this liquid to the sauce. Season and set aside to cool with a circle of greaseproof paper on top of the sauce.

Preheat the oven to 200°C (400°F, gas 6). Spoon half the mushrooms into the bottom of a deep 23 cm (9 in) square baking dish and cover with 3 crepes, trimming as necessary. Top with half the sauce. Repeat with remaining mushrooms, crepes and sauce. Sprinkle with the cheese, stand the dish on a baking tray and bake for 30–35 minutes until golden and bubbling. Serve immediately.

Spiced red cabbage with blackberries and apple

An interesting combination of seasonal flavours which makes the perfect side dish to accompany rich game birds or meats such as pheasant, grouse, duck or venison.

Serves 4–6

25 g (1 oz) unsalted butter
1 medium onion, peeled and chopped
1 bay leaf
1 small cinnamon stick, broken
¼ tsp ground nutmeg
500 g (1 lb 2 oz) red cabbage, trimmed and shredded
250 g (9 oz) cooking apples, peeled, cored and thinly sliced
4 tbsp blackberry or raspberry vinegar
50 g (2 oz) light brown sugar
150 g (5 oz) blackberries, washed and hulled
½ tsp salt
Freshly ground black pepper

Melt the butter in a large saucepan and gently fry the onion with the bay leaf and spices, for 5 minutes until softened but not browned.

Stir in the cabbage, apples, vinegar and sugar and mix well to thoroughly coat in the onion mixture. Bring to the boil, cover and simmer gently for 30 minutes. Add the blackberries, re-cover and continue coking for a further 10 minutes until tender. Discard the cinnamon and bay leaf, and season well before serving.

Cauliflower and broccoli gratin

We used to have cauliflower cheese for supper when I was a child and it was one of my favourites, served with thick slices of gammon or sausages. The secret is to use a really tasty cheese so it's worth investigating the mature farmhouse cheeses made in your area.

Serves 4

1 medium cauliflower, trimmed
225 g (8 oz) broccoli
Salt and freshly ground black pepper
4 rashers smoked streaky bacon, chopped
1 small onion, peeled and finely chopped
2 tbsp cornflour
600 ml (20 fl oz) whole milk
1 tbsp wholegrain mustard
175 g (6 oz) farmhouse Cheddar cheese or similar, grated
50 g (2 oz) fresh white breadcrumbs
25 g (1 oz) butter

Cut the cauliflower into small florets, and do the same with the broccoli, trimming the stalks as necessary. Bring a large saucepan of lightly salted water to the boil and cook the florets for 5–6 minutes until just tender. Drain well and allow to dry for 10 minutes. Preheat the oven to 200°C (400°F, gas 6).

Dry fry the bacon with the onion for 5–6 minutes, stirring, until softened but not browned. In a small bowl, mix the cornflour with a little of the milk to make a paste. Pour the milk on to the bacon and onion and then stir in the cornflour paste. Heat, stirring, until the mixture comes to the boil, then cook for 1 minute until thick. Remove from the heat and stir in the mustard and 115 g (4 oz) of the cheese.

Arrange the cooked cauliflower and broccoli evenly in an ovenproof gratin dish and spoon over the sauce. Mix the remaining cheese with the breadcrumbs and sprinkle over the top. Dot with butter and stand the dish on a baking tray. Bake in the oven for about 25 minutes until golden and bubbling. Serve immediately.

Slow roast onions with goat's cheese

Often neglected as an accompaniment vegetable, the onion can be transformed in to a sweet, meltingly tender delight cooked this way. Serve simply topped with fried breadcrumbs and some crumbled goat's cheese.

Serves 4

4 large brown onions
4 tsp light brown sugar
Salt and freshly ground black pepper
75 g (3 oz) butter
2 tbsp sunflower oil
50 g (2 oz) fresh white breadcrumbs
50 g (2 oz) crumbly goat's cheese
2 tbsp freshly chopped chives

Preheat the oven to 180°C (350°F, gas 4). Slice the tops off the onions and reserve, but do not peel. Carefully top each onion with a teaspoon of sugar and some seasoning. Cut 25 g (1 oz) butter into 4 pieces and place a piece of butter on top of each onion. Press the tops back on the onions and wrap each completely in foil.

Stand in a small roasting tin and bake in the oven for about 1½–2 hours until tender. Five minutes before the end of cooking, melt the remaining butter with the oil in a frying pan until bubbling and then stir fry the breadcrumbs for 5 minutes until golden.

Open the foil, remove the lids and cut a deep cross in the top. Scatter lightly with a few crumbs, some crumbled goat's cheese and a few chives. Rewrap in foil and bake in the oven for a further 10 minutes to warm through. Discard the foil and serve immediately – scoop out the flesh from the skins to eat – ideal with fish, poultry or sausages.

Baked mushrooms with haggis and sweet and sour sauce

Choose field mushrooms with a good cupped top about 7 cm (3 in) in diameter for this recipe. Replace the haggis with a slice of black pudding or sausagemeat if preferred – it makes a great breakfast dish!

Serves 4

1 tbsp cold pressed rapeseed oil
8 x 50 g (2 oz) slices haggis
8 small deep cupped field mushrooms, peeled and stalks removed
8 x rashers rindless lean unsmoked back bacon

For the sa
1 strip orange rind, cut into thin shreds
1 strip lemon rind, cut into thin shreds
4 tbsp boiling water
4 tbsp fruit jelly such as redcurrant (see pages 153)
2 tbsp red wine vinegar
¼ tsp ground ginger
Pinch of salt

Preheat the oven to 200°C (400°F, gas 6). Drizzle the oil over the base of a small shallow roasting tin. Trim the haggis to fit snugly inside the cups of the mushrooms and wrap a rasher of bacon around each mushroom, ensuring the ends meet underneath.

Place in the roasting tin and bake for 30–35 minutes, basting occasionally with any juices, until tender and cooked through.

Meanwhile, make the sauce. Put the orange and lemon rind in a small heatproof dish and spoon over the water. Soak for 5 minutes before transferring to a saucepan. Add the redcurrant jelly and heat gently until melted. Stir in the remaining ingredients, bring to the boil and simmer for 2 minutes. Set aside until ready to serve.

Serve the mushrooms with freshly cooked vegetables, accompanied with the sweet and sour sauce.

Forestière potatoes

Little potatoes baked in their skins taste sweet and earthy. They roast well with the flavours of thyme, garlic and mushrooms. A great alternative to the traditional roast vegetables.

Serves 4–6

225 g (8 oz) shallots
4 garlic cloves
450 g (1 lb) small potatoes in their skins, scrubbed
4 field mushrooms
A few sprigs fresh thyme
4 tbsp cold pressed rapeseed oil
Salt and freshly ground black pepper

Preheat the oven to 200°C (400°F, gas 6). Peel the shallots, cut in half lengthways and place in a bowl. Peel the garlic and cut into thick slices and toss into the shallots along with the potatoes.

Peel the mushrooms and cut into thick wedges. Carefully mix into the other vegetables along with the thyme. Spoon in the oil and carefully mix all the vegetables in the bowl until they are coated in oil.

Spread out evenly in a shallow roasting tin and season well. Bake in the oven for about 40 minutes, turning occasionally, until tender and golden. Discard the thyme before serving.

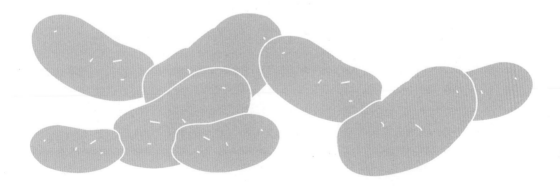

Blackberry meringue crush with sweet cider apple sauce

If we've had a good summer, the hedgerows will be full of these black jewels. This is one of the best free foods you can find, just be sure of your source and avoid blackberries from areas where crop spraying has taken place or next to a heavy polluting road.

Serves 4

2 free range egg whites
Pinch of salt
200 g (7 oz) light brown sugar, crushed to be free of lumps
225 g (8 oz) blackberries, washed and hulled
150 ml (5 fl oz) sweet cider or fresh apple juice
250 g (9 oz) cooking apples with a floury texture such as Bramley
2 tbsp freshly squeezed lemon juice
150 ml (5 fl oz) whipping cream

Preheat the oven to 130°C (250°F, gas ½). Line a baking sheet with baking parchment. In a large grease-free bowl, whisk the egg whites and salt until very dry and stiff. Gradually whisk in 115 g (4 oz) sugar, a spoonful at a time, until the mixture is stiff and glossy.

Drop 8 spoonfuls of meringue on to the prepared sheet and bake in the oven for about 3 hours until dried out and crisp. Allow to cool.

Meanwhile, put the blackberries in a saucepan with the remaining sugar and the cider. Bring to the boil, cover and simmer for 5 minutes until tender. Allow to cool, then strain the blackberries, reserving the cooking liquid, and cover and chill until required.

Peel, core and chop the apples. Place in a saucepan and toss in the lemon juice. Heat gently until steaming, then cover and simmer gently for about 5 minutes until soft and collapsed. Remove from the heat and push through a nylon sieve. Stir in reserved blackberry cooking juices to make a pouring sauce and set aside to cool.

To serve, whip the cream until just peaking. Put 2 meringues in each serving bowl and lightly crush. Top with whipped cream, a few cooked blackberries and pour over the apple sauce. Serve immediately.

Bonfire night toffee apples

Homemade toffee apples for bonfire night are so much nicer than the ones you can buy ready made. Choose your favourite eating apple variety, a good crisp crunchy one will give best results.

Makes 6

6 medium sized eating apples
225 g (8 oz) granulated sugar
2 tbsp golden syrup
1 tsp cider vinegar

Line a tray with a sheet of baking parchment and set aside. Wash the apples and pat dry with kitchen paper. Remove the stalks and push in clean ice lolly sticks or thick wooden skewers where the stalk used to be.

Put the sugar in a saucepan along with the syrup and vinegar. Heat gently, stirring until dissolved. Bring to the boil and cook without stirring for 5–6 minutes until it turns to rich golden caramel. Working quickly, holding each apple by the stick, carefully dip each one into the caramel, turning it until well coated. Leave to stand on the lined tray until completely cool and set. Best eaten on the same day as making.

Crumble topped plum pie

I couldn't decide whether to include a classic pie or crumble in this section, so I've combined the two together. You can make this recipe using rhubarb or apples, or in Summer, try it with gooseberries.

Serves 10

For the pastry and crumble:
350 g (12 oz) plain flour
½ tsp salt
225 g (8 oz) unsalted butter, cut into
    small pieces
3 tbsp caster sugar
115 g (4 oz) ground almonds
Approx. 2 tbsp cold water

For the filling:
900 g (2 lb) plums, quartered and stoned
75 g (3 oz) caster sugar
2 tbsp cornflour
1 tsp ground cinnamon
2 tsp icing sugar, for dusting

Grease and flour a 23 cm (9 in) spring-form cake tin. First make the pastry and crumble. Sieve the flour and salt in to a bowl, and rub in the butter until the mixture resembles fresh breadcrumbs. Stir in 2 tbsp sugar and the ground almonds. Weigh out 200 g (7 oz) of the mixture for the crumble topping, and stir the remaining sugar into this. Cover and chill until required.

To the remaining mixture, add sufficient water to bring the mixture together to form a firm pastry dough. Turn on to a lightly floured surface and knead gently until smooth. Wrap and chill for 30 minutes.

Roll out the pastry on a lightly floured surface to form a circle large enough to fit the base and sides of the tin. Carefully transfer the pastry to the tin and press in gently to fit evenly up the sides of the tin. Trim and chill for 30 minutes. Preheat the oven to 200°C (400°F, gas 6).

For the filling, mix the sugar, cornflour and cinnamon together and sprinkle 2 Tbsp over the base of the pastry case. Layer the plums in the pastry shell sprinkling with spiced sugar and cornflour as you go. Sprinkle the reserved crumble on top. Transfer to a baking tray and bake in the oven for about 1 hour, covering the top with foil if necessary to prevent over-browning. Stand for 15 minutes before removing from the tin and transferring to a large serving plate with a lip. Dust with icing sugar and serve hot or cold with custard – slice carefully as their will be lots of juice if served hot.

Mulled wine pear syllabub

A classic way to cook pears with a selection of warming spices and a good drop of red wine. If you use the cooking syrup to make a syllabub you'll have the perfect accompaniment too.

Serves 4

4 ripe pears
1 small stick cinnamon
1 bay leaf
1 strip pared orange rind
4 cloves
50 g (2 oz) light brown sugar
300 ml (10 fl oz) red wine
300 ml (10 fl oz) double cream
Ground cinnamon to dust

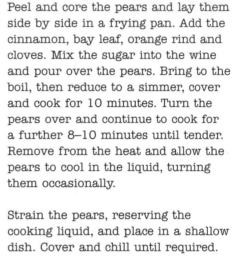

Peel and core the pears and lay them side by side in a frying pan. Add the cinnamon, bay leaf, orange rind and cloves. Mix the sugar into the wine and pour over the pears. Bring to the boil, then reduce to a simmer, cover and cook for 10 minutes. Turn the pears over and continue to cook for a further 8–10 minutes until tender. Remove from the heat and allow the pears to cool in the liquid, turning them occasionally.

Strain the pears, reserving the cooking liquid, and place in a shallow dish. Cover and chill until required. Strain the cooking liquid into a saucepan, bring to the boil and cook rapidly for 5–6 minutes until reduced by half and slightly syrupy. Allow to cool completely.

When ready to serve, pour the cream into a mixing bowl and begin whisking. At the same time, gradually pour in the red wine syrup. Continue whisking until just peaking. Arrange pear halves in serving dishes and pile the syllabub on top. Dust with ground cinnamon and serve immediately.

Tip: You can prepare the syllabub up to 30 minutes in advance and keep in the refrigerator. After this time, the juices may begin to separate from the cream.

Chocolate raspberry squidgy cakes

Popular with my female tasters, these dense cakes are best served warm. Autumn raspberries are full of flavour and mixed into a treacly chocolate sponge they are a real comfort fix when there's a nip in the air. If you don't eat them all at once, they freeze well.

Makes 12

200 g (7 oz) self raising flour
25 g (1 oz) cocoa powder
115 g (4 oz) dark brown sugar, crushed to be free of lumps
115 g (4 oz) plain chocolate chips
2 medium free range eggs, beaten
150 ml (5 fl oz) whole milk
115 g (4 oz) butter, melted
1 tsp good quality vanilla extract
200 g (7 oz) fresh raspberries

Preheat the oven to 180°C (350°F, gas 4). Place 12 paper muffin cases in deep cup muffin tins.

Sift the flour and cocoa into a bowl, stir in the sugar and chocolate chips and make a well in the centre. Mix the eggs, milk, melted butter and vanilla together and pour into the well, stirring to form a stiff batter, but taking care not to over mix. Carefully fold in the raspberries.

Divide the batter between the muffin cases. Smooth the tops slightly and bake in then oven for about 40 minutes, until risen to the top of the cases and just set in the centre. Transfer to a wire rack to cool.

Best served warm on day of baking.

Fragrant slow-baked quince

Quince is a fruit that I use as much as cooking apples when in season in the Autumn. I like the firmer texture, and sourer, pronounced flavour, and the beautiful colour which it magically turns on cooking.

Serves 6

Juice of 1 lemon
1 kg (2 lb 3½ oz) quince
Pinch of saffron
1 vanilla pod, split
2 tbsp strong tasting local honey, such as heather
300 ml (10 fl oz) boiling water
Rose water, to taste, optional

Preheat the oven to 150°C (300°F, gas 2). Put the lemon juice in a bowl and half fill with cold water. Peel and core the quince and cut into thick wedges or quarters, depending on size, putting them in the lemony water as soon as possible.

In a heatproof jug, put the saffron, vanilla and honey and pour over the boiling water. Stir until the honey dissolves.

Drain the quince and place in an ovenproof dish with a well fitting lid. Pour over the spiced honey water, cover with foil and replace the lid. Bake in the oven for 2–2½ hours, turning after an hour, until rich peachy pink in colour and tender. Remove the lid, and loosen the foil, and allow to cool in the liquid. Discard the vanilla.

Best served at room temperature, sprinkled with rose water if liked, and accompanied with thick whole milk yogurt or whipped cream.

Spiced pear and blackberry cake

Blackberries can have quite a perfumed flavour about them, and mixing them with pear and subtle spices, helps bring it out. This is a really hearty cake, ideal served in hunks with a cup of hot steaming tea.

Serves 8–10

150 g (5 oz) unsalted butter, softened
150 g (5 oz) light brown sugar
3 free range eggs, beaten
250 g (9 oz) plain flour
1 tbsp baking powder
1½ tsp mixed spice
1 tsp vanilla extract
350 g (12 oz) ripe pears, peeled, cored and finely chopped
175 g (6 oz) blackberries, hulled and well washed
3 tbsp Demerara sugar

Preheat the oven to 170°C (325°F, gas 3). Grease and line a deep 20 cm (8 in) round cake tin.

In a mixing bowl, cream together the butter and light brown sugar until paler in colour and creamy in texture. Gradually whisk in the eggs with 4 tbsp flour. Sieve in the remaining flour along with the baking powder and mixed spice; fold in carefully along with the vanilla extract, chopped pears and blackberries.

Pile into the prepared tin and smooth the top. Sprinkle with the Demerara sugar. Bake in the oven for about 1¼ hours until risen and golden, and a skewer inserted into the centre comes out clean. Leave to cool in tin for 10 minutes before turning on to a wire rack to cook completely. Wrap and store for 24 hours to allow the flavours to develop, before slicing to serve.

Squash and treacle tart

Over the years, golden syrup has replaced the dark sticky molasses-based treacle of days gone by in many desserts. This is my version of an American Hallowe'en favourite which is also good served cold.

Serves 8

300 g (10 oz) readymade sweet shortcrust pastry
50 g (2 oz) unsalted butter
150 ml (5 fl oz) golden syrup
2 free range eggs, beaten
300 g (10 oz) cooked, cold mashed squash or pumpkin
Pinch of salt
1 tsp ground cinnamon

Preheat the oven to 180°C (350°F, gas 4). On a lightly floured surface roll out the pastry to fit a 23 cm (9 in) loose-bottomed flan tin, trim and chill until required.

Meanwhile, make the filling. Put the butter in a saucepan with the syrup and heat gently until melted – do not allow to boil. Cool for 10 minutes then beat in the eggs and mashed squash. Add a pinch of salt and stir in the cinnamon. Push through a sieve into a jug to make a smooth purée.

Put the pastry case on a baking sheet and pour in the filling. Bake in the oven for about 50 minutes until set. Leave to cool in the tin for 10 minutes, then transfer to a serving plate. Serve hot or cold with ice cream.

As I sit here typing away on an unseasonably wet and miserable July day, it seems fitting that I'm writing about Winter. When I think of this season, my first thoughts are of hearty stews with melt-in-the-mouth tender meat, intense flavours and lots of hearty root vegetables.

WINTER

(December, January, February)

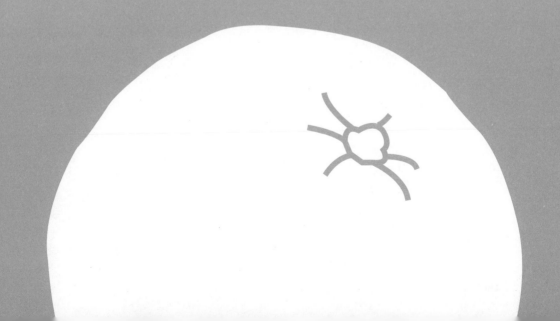

There's not much going on in the garden during these months for the fruit and vegetable grower, so this is the time of year we come to rely on the hardier vegetables and stored produce harvested in the Autumn. It's also a great time to root through the freezer and find some of that lovely Spring and Summer produce you put away for such an occasion. In season this month are vegetables like parsnips, swede, turnip, celeriac and Jerusalem artichokes. Greenery is stronger tasting and makes the ideal accompaniment for rich flavoured meat dishes; you'll find Brussels sprouts, curly kale and Winter cabbage all good to go with roast meat and casseroles.

When it comes to fruit, there are plenty of apples and pears around, and also quince, another of my favourites, might still be around if stored. It makes an interesting substitute for either apple or pear and adds a rich pinky orange colour and perfumed flavour to pies and bakes, and also makes an unusual accompaniment to serve with game meats which are still widely available – mutton is making a come back and makes an excellent choice for long slow cooking. Its meaty flavour goes well with robust ingredients – try the curry on page 117. And, of course, at the end of the year we celebrate Christmas, so there will be bountiful supplies of turkey, and goose, for those who want to step back in time – see page 119 for a traditional roast recipe straight out of the pages of Charles Dickens!

Let's not forget fish. Scallops, langoustines, oysters, turbot and salmon are excellent choices for Christmas starters or lighter festive meals, and add to the celebratory feel in the air.

Finally, a little reminder that Spring is on its way, towards the end of Winter you'll start to see the pink stems of forced rhubarb in the greengrocer's. The tender stems cook in next to no time and are a welcome and refreshing flavour after all the richness of Christmas and overindulgence.

Apples (cooking): Bramley (dessert): Spartan/Cox's Orange Pippin/Ida/Red/Laxton Superb/Crispin/Golden Delicious	
Brussels sprouts	
Cabbages: Spring greens/Savoy/Winter White	until April
Red	until January
Spring cabbage	new season from February to May
Celery	until February
Celeriac	
Chicory	all year but at best from November to April
Endive	all year but at best from November to April
Horseradish	
Jerusalem artichoke	
Kale	
Kohlrabi	
Leeks	
Onions: maincrop	
Parsnips	
Pears	
Potatoes: maincrop	
Rhubarb: forced	new season from December to March
Salsify	
Sea Kale	new season from December to March
Shallots	
Swede	
Turnips	

MEAT: goose, grouse, guinea fowl, hare, mutton, partridge, pheasant, rabbit, venison, teal, turkey, wild duck, wood pigeon
FISH: brill, clams, cockles, halibut, hake, John Dory, lemon sole, langoustines, monkfish, mussels, oysters, plaice, scallops, sea bass, turbot

UK produce available all year:

FRUIT & VEGETABLES
Beetroot
Broccoli
Carrots – except May and June
Cauliflower
Chicory
Endive
Garlic
Herbs (greenhouse)
Lettuces and salad leaves (greenhouse)
Mushrooms – white, button, brown and flat
Mustard and cress
Spinach
Spring onions

MEAT
beef, chicken, pork

FISH
cod, coley, haddock, queen scallops (farmed), salmon (farmed) scallops, skate, whiting, winkles

Root vegetable pottage

It's not often you get to serve up a bright pink dish, but by adding beetroot to the mix, you'll end up with a vibrant coloured soup that tastes wholesome and hearty. It is advisable to wear rubber gloves when you grate beetroot to help prevent staining your fingers.

Serves 4

2 tbsp sunflower oil
2 tsp coriander seeds, lightly crushed
1 large red onion, peeled and chopped
300 g (10 oz) beetroot, peeled and grated
300 g (10 oz) potatoes, peeled and diced
225 g (8 oz) celeriac, peeled and diced
225 g (8 oz) carrots, peeled and diced
1.2 l (40 fl oz) fresh vegetable stock (see page 156)
Salt and freshly ground black pepper
6 tbsp whole milk yogurt
1 tsp caraway seeds

Heat the oil in a large saucepan and fry the coriander seeds for 2 minutes. Add the onion and beetroot and cook for a further 5 minutes to soften without browning. Add the remaining vegetables and pour over the stock. Bring to the boil and simmer for 20 minutes until tender.

Using a slotted spoon, transfer the vegetables to a blender or food processor, reserving the cooking liquid. Add 2 ladlefuls of the cooking liquid and blend until smooth,

Return to the saucepan and stir in the remaining cooking liquid. Add 4 tbsp yogurt and season well. Heat, stirring, for 3–4 minutes until hot but not boiling. Ladle into warmed serving bowls, top each with a small spoonful of the remaining yogurt and sprinkle with caraway seeds to serve.

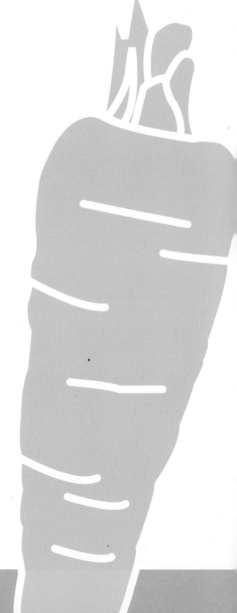

Mutton and barley broth

For slow cooking, I think mutton beats lamb hands down. It is much meatier, and adds great flavour to the humblest of ingredients.

Serves 6

2 tbsp sunflower oil
500 g (1 lb 2 oz) trimmed boneless shoulder or leg of mutton, and cut into 1 cm (½ in) thick pieces
1 tsp cumin seeds, lightly crushed
1 onion, peeled and finely chopped
2 sticks celery, trimmed and diced
1 large carrot, peeled and diced
1 small swede (turnip), peeled and diced
2 sprigs rosemary
2 fresh or 1 dried bay leaf
1.5 l (50 fl oz) fresh lamb stock (see page 156)
100 g (3½ oz) pearl barley, rinsed
Salt and freshly ground black pepper

Heat half the oil in a large saucepan and gently fry the mutton with the cumin seeds, stirring, for 3–4 minutes until browned all over. Remove from the saucepan, on to a plate using a slotted spoon, whilst you fry the vegetables.

Heat the remaining oil in the same saucepan and fry the vegetables for 5 minutes until softened but not brown. Return the mutton to the pan and add the herbs and pour over the stock. Bring to the boil, reduce to a gentle simmer, cover and cook for about 1½ hours until tender. Add the pearl barley, bring back to the boil, cover and continue to cook as before, for a further 50 minutes until the barley is swollen and tender. Discard the herbs and season well.

Ladle in to warmed soup bowls. Serve immediately with bread to mop up the stock.

Spanish-style oxtail stew with chilli dough boys

Rich beefy stew and dumplings is perfect for a Winter's day. Cook really slowly so that the meat is meltingly tender. Incidentally, 'dough boys' is our quaint family name for dumplings!

Serves 4

1.35 kg (3 lb) oxtail pieces
Salt and freshly ground black pepper
2 tbsp plain flour
175 g (6 oz) chorizo sausage, chopped
2 tbsp sunflower oil
2 medium onion, peeled and chopped
2 cloves garlic, peeled and chopped
450 g (1 lb) carrots, peeled and thickly sliced
4 strips pared orange rind
2 tsp sweet smoked or plain sweet paprika
500 ml (17 fl oz) Spanish red wine
400 ml (14 fl oz) fresh beef stock (see page 156)
2 bay leaves
1 sprig rosemary

For the dumplings:
175 g (6 oz) self raising flour
2 tbsp freshly chopped rosemary
½ tsp cayenne pepper
75 g (3 oz) beef suet
Approx. 150 ml (5 fl oz) cold water

Wash and pat dry the oxtail. Season the flour and then use to lightly coat the oxtail pieces. Heat a large saucepan until hot and then dry fry the chorizo for 2–3 minutes until the juices run. Remove using a slotted spoon and set aside. Add the sunflower oil to the pan juices and heat, then fry the oxtail pieces, reserving any leftover seasoned flour, turning, until browned all over. Remove the oxtail and set aside. Gently fry the onions and garlic in the oils for about 5 minutes until softened but not browned.

Return the oxtail, chorizo and reserved seasoned flour to the saucepan and add the carrots. Stir together over the heat for one minute before adding the remaining ingredients, except those for the dumplings. Bring to the boil, cover and reduce to a gentle simmer and cook for 3½ hours or until the meat falls off the bone and the sauce is richly thickened. Discard the orange peel and herbs

For the dumplings, sift the flour into a bowl and stir in the rosemary, cayenne pepper and suet. Season well and stir in sufficient water to form a soft dough. Lightly flour your hands and work surface and knead the dough lightly. Form into 8 equal portions and shape into balls.

Arrange the dumplings round the edge of the saucepan, re-cover and continue to cook for a further 30 minutes until the dumplings are risen and cooked through. Serve the stew with mashed potatoes and green vegetables.

Mutton, potato and spinach curry

Another fantastic Winter warmer. With long slow cooking, mutton will be tender and succulent, and is robust enough in flavour to stand up well with the addition of Indian spices.

Serves 4

1 tsp coriander seeds, lightly crushed
1 tsp mustard seeds, lightly crushed
6 cardamom pods, green casing removed and seeds lightly crushed
1 small onion, peeled and chopped
2 garlic cloves, peeled and chopped
2.5 cm (1 in) piece root ginger, peeled and chopped
2 fleshy mild green chillies, deseeded and chopped
2 tbsp vegetable oil
675 g (1½ lb) trimmed boneless shoulder or leg of mutton, cut into 2-cm (¾-in) pieces
400 ml (14 oz) can coconut milk
500 g (1 lb 2oz) firm potatoes, such as Maris Piper, peeled and cut into 2 cm (¾-in) thick pieces
225 g (8 oz) spinach, trimmed
1 tsp salt
4 tbsp freshly chopped coriander

Put the seeds and cardamom in a small frying pan and heat, stirring, for 3–4 minutes until lightly toasted and fragrant. Set aside. Place the onion, garlic, ginger and chillies in a blender or food processor. Add the toasted spices and 1 tbsp oil and blend for a few seconds to make a paste.

Heat the remaining oil in a large saucepan and gently fry the paste for 3 minutes until softened but not browned. Add the mutton and cook, stirring, for 2–3 minutes until well coated in the paste.

Pour over the coconut milk. Bring to the boil, then cover and simmer gently for 1½ hours. Stir in the potatoes, bring back to the boil, cover and continue to simmer gently for a further hour until tender.

Wash and pat dry the spinach. Add the spinach to the curry in batches, stirring well after each addition. Stir in the salt, cover and continue to cook for about 10 minutes, stirring occasionally, until the spinach is wilted and very soft and the sauce is thick. Sprinkle generously with the chopped coriander and serve immediately.

Gammon and apple cobbler

This is a really British dish. Often made with fruit and served as a pudding, this savoury version is filling and comforting. You can make it with sausages or minced pork instead of the gammon if preferred.

Serves 4

1 tbsp sunflower oil
25 g (1 oz) butter
1 medium onion, peeled and chopped
2 sticks celery, trimmed and sliced
2 eating apples, peeled, cored and thickly sliced
450 g (1 lb) lean unsmoked gammon, trimmed and cut into 2 cm (¾ in) pieces
1 tbsp freshly chopped sage
300 ml (10 fl oz) fresh ham or chicken stock – see page 156
150 ml (5 fl oz) dry cider or freshly pressed apple juice
Salt and freshly ground black pepper
2 tbsp cornflour
2 tbsp double cream

For the topping:
225 g (8 oz) self raising flour
½ tsp salt
50 g (2 oz) butter
120 ml (4 fl oz) whole milk plus extra for glazing

Heat the oil and butter in a large saucepan until bubbling and fry the onion, celery, and apples for 5 minutes until softened but not browned. Add the gammon and continue to cook, stirring, for a further 5 minutes until the gammon is browned all over.

Add the sage and pour over the stock and cider or apple juice. Bring to the boil and simmer for 10 minutes. Blend the cornflour with the cream to form a paste, and stir into the gammon mixture. Cook, stirring, for 2 minutes until the sauce has thickened. Spoon into a large oval gratin dish and set aside. Preheat the oven to 200°C (400°F, gas 6).

For the topping, sieve the flour and salt into a bowl and rub in the butter until the mixture resembles fresh breadcrumbs. Bind together with sufficient milk to bind together to form a softish dough. Turn on to a lightly floured surface and knead gently until smooth. Roll the dough to a thickness of 1 cm (½ in) and using a 5 cm (2 in) round cutter, stamp out 9 or 10 rounds, re-rolling as necessary. Arrange the scones around the edge of the dish, overlapping a little. Put the dish on a baking tray and glaze the topping lightly with a little milk. Bake in the oven for about 25 minutes until the topping is risen and lightly golden. Serve immediately with freshly cooked vegetables.

Christmas roast goose with sage and onion stuffing

In days gone by, the goose was 'the' bird for your festive lunch, and in recent years, this delicious roast has seen a resurgence in popularity. For all its size, the yield is quite low, but the flesh is flavoursome and a real treat for the season.

Serves 8

4 medium onions, peeled and chopped
600 ml (20 fl oz) vegetable stock
4 tbsp freshly chopped sage
175 g (6 oz) fresh white breadcrumbs
75 g (3 oz) butter
Salt and freshly ground black pepper
4–5.5 kg (9–12 lb) oven-ready goose,
    giblets removed
8 small cooking apples
75 g (3 oz) no-need-to-soak dried prunes,
    finely chopped
25 g (1 oz) walnuts, chopped
½ tsp ground cinnamon
Fresh sage to garnish

Preheat the oven to 190°C (375°F, gas 5). First make the stuffing. Place the onions in a saucepan. Pour over the stock and bring to the boil. Simmer for 10 minutes until very soft. Drain well – reserve the onion stock for your gravy – and cool for 10 minutes before blending in a food processor until smooth.

Transfer to a large bowl and stir in the chopped sage, bread crumbs and 50 g (2 oz) butter. Season well and mix until the butter melts. Set aside to cool.

For the goose, pull out the lumps of fat from inside the goose and set aside. Prick the skin all over with a fork. Season and lay some of the fat from the cavity on the thighs to keep them moist. Cover with foil and place on a rack over a roasting tin in the oven and regularly empty the fat. Calculate the cooking time as follows:
4 kg (9 lb) goose will take 3 hours, 4.5–5 kg (10–11 lb) will take 3½ hours, and a 5.5 kg (12 lb) goose will take 4 hours. Remove the foil for 30–40 minutes before the end of cooking so that the skin can brown. To test for doneness, pierce the fattest part of the thigh with a skewer; the juices will run clear if the goose is cooked.

Put the stuffing into a greased small shallow roasting tin and cook along side the goose for the last 40 minutes of cooking.

For the apples, core the apples and score the skin around the middle of each. Mix the prunes with the walnuts and cinnamon and press into each apple. Place in a small baking dish and top each with a knob of the remaining butter. Place in the oven and cook for the last 30 minutes of the goose's cooking time.

Drain the goose and allow to stand for 15 minutes. Transfer to a warm serving platter and arrange the cooked apples around. Spoon the stuffing into mounds and arrange round the goose along with lots of fresh sage. Serve with redcurrant jelly.

Haggis, neeps and tattie pies

Scotland has a great pie heritage, and these little gems can be found all over the country in baker's and butcher's shops alike. This is my version, great as a hot on-the-hoof snack or served with gravy and vegetables as a main meal.

Makes 6

450 g (1 lb) plain flour
½ tsp salt
100 g (3½ oz) unsalted butter
75 g (3 oz) lard
175 ml (6 fl oz) water
225 g (8 oz) haggis
225 g (8 oz) piece swede (turnip), peeled and grated
225 g (8 oz) potato, peeled and grated
Salt and freshly ground pepper
1 free range egg, beaten, to glaze

Sieve the flour and salt into a heatproof bowl and make a well in the centre. Put the butter, lard and water in a saucepan and heat gently to melt, then turn up the heat until simmering. Pour into the well and mix to form a smooth dough. Knead on a lightly floured surface until smooth and elastic, the place back in the bowl, cover and allow to stand in a warm place for about 30 minutes – don't allow the dough to cool completely.

Preheat the oven to 200°C (400°F, gas 6). Roll two thirds of the pastry on a lightly floured surface and using a saucer, stamp out 6 x 15 cm (6 in) rounds, re-rolling as necessary, and press into 6 x 10 cm (4 in) large cup muffin tins. Roll out the remaining pastry and stamp out 6 x 10 cm (4 in) rounds for the lids, re-rolling as necessary. Divide the haggis between the bases of each pastry case, and top with a layer of swede and then potato, seasoning as you layer, and packing down well. Brush the edge of the pastry with egg and press the pastry lids on top. Press the edges together to seal. Make a hole in the top of each and brush the tops with egg. Bake for 30 minutes then reduce the temperature to 180°C (350°F, gas 4) and cook for a further 20 minutes until golden and the filling is tender. Cool in the tin for 5 minutes then transfer to a wire rack. Serve hot with gravy or cool for a bit longer and serve warm.

Liver and onions with colcannon mash

I admit to being put off all types of offal because of bad memories of school dinners when the liver was strong tasting and cooked until the texture of leather – yuk! However, I've got over my fears now, and suggest choosing calf's or lamb's liver combined with light cooking which makes a much nicer dish.

Serves 2

2 tbsp cold pressed rapeseed oil
50 g (2 oz) butter
2 medium onions, peeled and thinly sliced
350 g (12 oz) potatoes, peeled and diced
Salt and freshly ground black pepper
115 g (4 oz) kale
2 tbsp milk
225 g (8 oz) calf's or lamb's liver, cut into thin slices
2 tbsp freshly chopped parsley

Heat half the oil with 15 g (½ oz) butter until bubbling and gently fry the onions, covered, for about 30 minutes, stirring occasionally until tender. Remove the lid, raise the temperature and cook for a further 2–3 minutes until golden.

Meanwhile, put the potatoes in a saucepan and cover with water. Add a pinch of salt, bring to the boil and cook for 10–12 minutes until tender. Drain well, return to the saucepan and mash. Cover and keep aside. Cut the curly kale leaves from the central stalks and chop roughly. Wash thoroughly and place in a saucepan without drying so that the kale will cook in the steam produced by the wet leaves. Cover and cook over a gentle heat for 10–12 minutes until tender. Drain well and chop finely.

Stir the kale into the mashed potato along with the milk and a knob of the remaining butter. Cover and keep warm.

When you are ready to serve, heat the remaining oil with the remaining butter in a frying pan and fry the liver over a high heat for 1–2 minutes, stirring, until sealed and but still pink. Pile the mashed on to warmed serving plates and top with onions and the liver. Sprinkle with parsley and serve immediately.

Venison and juniper pie

Now farmed all year round, lean, richly flavoured venison lends itself well to the flavours and cooking of Winter months. This is a truly gamey pie but you could use lean beef steak if you prefer.

Serves 4–6

900 g (2 lb) boneless shoulder of venison, cut into 2.5 cm (1 in) pieces
Salt and freshly ground black pepper
3 tbsp plain flour
25 g (1 oz) butter
2 tbsp sunflower oil
2 medium onions, peeled and chopped
2 carrots, peeled and sliced
1 tbsp juniper berries, crushed
200 ml (7 fl oz) red wine
450 ml (15 fl oz) fresh beef stock (see page 156)
2 bay leaves
2 sprigs thyme
2 tbsp red wine vinegar
2 tbsp dark brown sugar
250 g (9 oz) puff pastry, thawed if frozen
1 free range egg, beaten, to glaze

First make the filling. Toss the venison in the seasoning and flour. Melt the butter in a large saucepan until bubbling and add the meat (keep any flour that remains). Cook, stirring, for about 5 minutes until browned all over. Remove from the pan using a slotted spoon and set aside.

Heat the oil in the same saucepan, add the onion and carrot to the saucepan and cook, stirring, for 3 minutes. Remove from the heat and add the juniper and stir in the wine and stock.

Return the venison to the saucepan and add the herbs and vinegar. Bring to the boil, reduce to a simmer, cover and cook gently for 1½–2 hours until tender. Discard the herbs, allow to cool then transfer to an 1.2 l (40 fl oz) oval pie dish. Preheat the oven to 220°C (425°F, gas 7).

Roll out the pastry on a lightly floured board to just larger than the pie dish. Carefully cut some of the excess pastry into thin strips and secure on to the edge of the pie dish with water. Brush with egg. Transfer the rolled out pastry to the top and press down on to the edge using a fork. Roll out the trimmings and stamp out decorations. Secure on top of the pie with beaten egg. Make a hole in the centre and brush all over with egg.

Put the dish on a baking tray and bake for 20 minutes, then reduce the temperature to 180°C (350°F, gas 4) and cook for a further 25–30 minutes until crisp, golden and hot. Serve immediately with freshly cooked vegetables.

Three bird roast

This dish takes a while to prepare but makes an interesting Christmas roast alternative. If you're feeling adventurous, try boning the birds yourself, otherwise get your butcher to do it for you, but remember to give him plenty of notice over the Christmas period.

Serves 8–10

250 g (9 oz) pork sausagemeat
50 g (2 oz) cooked peeled chestnuts, finely chopped
1 tsp freshly chopped thyme leaves
Salt and freshly ground black pepper
Approx. 2.7 kg (6 lb) large chicken or small turkey, boned, skin on
Approx. 1.8 kg (5 lb) Gressingham duck, boned, skin removed
Approx. 900g (2 lb) pheasant, boned, skin removed
25 g (1 oz) butter, softened
8 rashers lean unsmoked back bacon

Preheat the oven to 190°C (375°F, gas 5). Place a roasting tin of water in the bottom of the oven as it heats up. In a bowl, mix together with sausagemeat, chestnut, thyme and seasoning.

Line a large board with clear wrap, unfold the chicken and lay on top of the clear wrap, skin-side down. Unroll the duck and lay neatly on top of the chicken, and finally lay the pheasant on top of the duck. Form the stuffing into a fat sausage and place down the centre of the meat.

Carefully bring up the sides of the meat and bacon over the stuffing to form a large rolled joint. Secure the ends together using skewers. Carefully turn the joint over and secure the roll in several places down its length with clean pieces of string. Remove the skewers. Weigh the rolled joint and calculate the cooking time as 25 minutes per 450 g (1 lb) plus and extra 25 minutes.

Put the rolled meat in a roasting tin. Thickly spread with butter and arrange the bacon rashers, overlapping, down the length of the meat, making sure it is well covered. Bake in the oven for the required time, basting frequently, and covering with foil for the last 45 minutes to prevent the meat over browning. Top up the water tray as necessary. Stand for 15 minutes before carving, and discard the bacon and remove string before serving.

Note: Use the cooking juices to make your accompanying gravy.

Hot pigeon with pear and red cabbage salad

Pigeon is most widely available in late Winter and its tasty, livery meat goes very well with the pepperiness of raw cabbage and light spices. Pear adds a touch of sweetness. If you can't get pigeons, this works well with quails. Take care not to overcook the birds as they will toughen – best served pink.

Serves 4

¼ red cabbage, core and outer leaves removed
1 small red onion, peeled and finely chopped
1 large carrot, peeled and coarsely grated
4 wood pigeon
Salt and freshly ground black pepper
6 tbsp cold pressed rapeseed oil
2 ripe pears
Juice of 1 lemon
¼ tsp cayenne pepper
¼ tsp ground cumin
2 tsp local clear honey
2 tbsp freshly chopped coriander

Finely shred the cabbage leaves an place in a bowl. Mix in the onion and carrot. Cover and chill until required.

Wash and pat dry the pigeons. Turn the birds breast-side down and using a sharp knife or heavy duty kitchen scissors, cut along the back bone from neck to tail, and then cut out the back bone along with the wish bone. Turn the birds over and flatten out completely using the heel of your hand to make a butterfly shape – this process is called spatch-cocking. Thread long skewers through from one side of the bird to the other, threading 2 pigeons between 2 skewers.

Preheat the grill to a medium/hot setting. Season the birds on both sides and place on the grill rack. Brush generously with 2 tbsp oil and cook for 7–8 minutes. Turn the birds over, brush with another 2 tbsp oil, and continue to cook for a further 7–8 minutes until just cooked, but still pink. Drain.

Meanwhile, peel and core the pears and slice thinly. Brush with a little lemon juice and set aside. Mix the remaining lemon juice with the remaining oil and season with cayenne and cumin. Whisk in the honey and plenty of salt and pepper. Toss into the cabbage mixture.

To serve, remove the skewers from the pigeons, pile the cabbage salad on to serving plates and top with a few slices of pear and then a freshly cooked pigeon. Sprinkle with coriander and serve immediately.

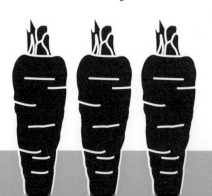

Black pudding and scallop salad

Unusual sounding at first reading, but scallop flesh is sweet and meaty and blends very well with the rich crumbly texture of black pudding. The bitter leaves and sweet apples are a perfect contrasting accompaniment.

Serves 4 as a starter

1 tbsp sunflower oil
4 generous slices black pudding
8 fresh scallops, removed from shells
Salt and freshly ground black pepper
50 g (2 oz) butter
2 eating apples, peeled, cored and thinly
    sliced
1 small head endive, washed and shaken
    dry

Heat the oil in a frying pan and gently fry the black pudding for 3–4 minutes on each side until just cooked through. Drain, reserving the juices and keep warm.

Wash and pat dry the scallops, and season on both sides. Add a knob of butter to the black pudding juices and heat until melted and bubbling. Cook the scallops for 1–2 minutes on each side until just cooked through. Drain and keep warm.

In another frying pan, melt the remaining butter until bubbling. Add the apples and cook quickly, stirring, for 2–3 minutes until just tender. Drain.

To serve, pile salad leaves on 4 small serving plates. Cut the black pudding into small pieces and sprinkle over the leaves. Slice the scallops and arrange on top, and finally top with a few slices of apple. Season and serve immediately.

Deep fried haddock and chips

To me, the best battered fish is haddock. I love the juicy flesh and fine, softer texture more than other white fish, so forget the local chippie and have a go at making your own fish supper.

Serves 4

900 g (2 lb) large firm-textured potatoes such as Maris Piper, Rooster or Golden Wonder
1 tsp salt
115 g (4 oz) plus 2 tbsp self raising flour
½ tsp baking powder
Sunflower oil for deep-frying
200 ml (7 fl oz) whole milk
4 x 175–225 g (6–8 oz) pieces haddock fillet

Peel the potatoes and cut into 1 cm (½ in) thick chip shapes. Rinse in cold running water. Place in a saucepan and cover with water. Add ½ tsp salt and bring to the boil. Cook for 6–7 minutes until almost cooked, but still firm. Drain well and set aside.

Sift 115 g (4 oz) flour into a bowl with the baking powder and ½ tsp salt. Make a well in the centre and add 2 tsp sunflower oil and gradually pour in the milk, whisking to make a batter the consistency of single cream. Set aside.

Heat the oil for deep-frying to reach 190°C (375°F). Fry the par-boiled chips for about 5 minutes until golden and crisp. Drain on kitchen paper and keep warm. Allow the oil to cool to 180°C (350°F).

Wash and pat dry the fish. Dust both sides of the fish with the remaining 2 tbsp flour, then dip in the prepared batter and place in the hot oil. Fry 2 pieces at a time for 5–6 minutes, turning halfway through, until the batter is crisp, golden and puffed up. Drain well and keep warm whilst cooking the other fish.

Serve the fish and chips with lemon wedges, and mayonnaise to accompany.

Buttered skate in parchment

Skate is often served with black butter and capers, but I prefer the flavour of fresh butter and the pungency of the pickles with my skate. Cooking in parchment is one of the best ways to preserve fish flavour and juices.

Serves 4

4 x 250 g (9 oz) skate wings, trimmed
Salt and freshly ground black pepper
65 g (2½ oz) unsalted butter
4 tbsp pickled capers, drained and rinsed
8 sprigs fresh tarragon

Preheat the oven to 200°C (400°F, gas 6). Wash and pat dry the skate. Cut 4 large sheets of baking parchment and place a skate wing in the centre of each. Season and top each with a knob of butter, 1 tbsp capers and a sprig of tarragon.

Seal the edges of the parchment around the fish by folding the edges together and pinching them to crease the paper completely shut. Put the parcels on a baking tray and bake for 20 minutes, undisturbed.

To serve, put each parcel on a warm serving plate and carry to the table along with the fresh tarragon. Once the parcels have been opened, scatter with a few fresh tarragon leaves. Accompany with freshly cooked vegetables and some bread to mop up the cooking juices.

Walnut and goat's cheese crusted cod

This dish is based on an idea of a locally sourced fresh pesto sauce. The robust flavour of walnuts is good with a meaty fish like cod and the goat's cheese adds a creaminess. I've used parsley as an obvious herb to go with fish, but it's worth experimenting with others, like dill.

Serves 4

115 g (4 oz) shelled walnuts
2 garlic cloves, peeled
6 tbsp walnut oil
15 g (½ oz) curly parsley
Salt and freshly ground black pepper
4 x 150 g (5 oz) skinless cod or other similar white fish fillets
75 g (3 oz) crumbly locally produced goat's cheese

Preheat the oven to 200°C (400°F, gas 6). Put the walnuts, garlic, 4 tbsp oil and parsley in a blender or food processor and blend well until smooth. Season well.

Wash and pat dry the cod fillets and season on both sides. Place on a baking tray lined with baking parchment. Spread the walnut paste thickly on top of each piece of cod and crumble over the goat's cheese. Drizzle with the remaining oil and bake in the oven for about 20 minutes until crusty and cooked through. Serve immediately with freshly cooked vegetables.

Roast langoustines with smoky garlic mayo

This makes a stunning dish to serve at a special celebration. Langoustines are sweet and succulent and are best served soon after roasting to enjoy these qualities at their best. Remember to put some finger bowls out for messy hands.

Serves 4

For the mayonnaise:
1 quantity mayonnaise (see page 154)
4 cloves smoked garlic, peeled and crushed
1 tsp smoked paprika
2 tbsp freshly chopped parsley

For the langoustines:
16 raw langoustines
Salt and freshly ground black pepper
4 tbsp cold pressed rapeseed oil

1 lemon, cut into wedges, to serve

Make up the mayonnaise as described on page 154 and mix in the garlic, paprika and parsley. Cover and chill until required.

Preheat the oven to 240°C (450°F, gas 8). Wash and pat dry the langoustines. Drizzle 1 tbsp oil on to small baking tray and arrange the langoustines on top. Brush them generously with the remaining oil and bake in the oven for 5 minutes. Stand for 10 minutes and then serve with wedges of lemon and the mayonnaise to dip.

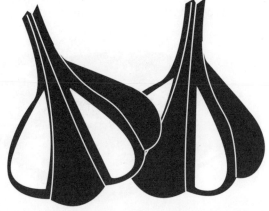

Moules with creamy garlic liquor

I'm including this dish because it's one of my favourite bistro shellfish dishes. If it's full of fishy garlicy flavour, nothing else comes close. I usually have chips and a salad to go with my mussels, and I always ask for a spoon to eat up all the liquor!

Serves 4

1.35 kg (3 lb) mussels, thoroughly cleaned
25 g (1 oz) unsalted butter
4 shallots, peeled and finely chopped
2 garlic cloves, peeled and finely chopped
200 ml (7 fl oz) dry white wine
200 ml (7 fl oz) fresh fish stock (see page 156)
4 tbsp freshly chopped parsley
5 tbsp double cream
Salt and freshly ground black pepper

Rinse the mussels well and make sure they are very clean. Melt the butter in a large saucepan and gently fry the shallots and garlic for 5 minutes until softened but not browned. Pour over the wine and stock. Bring to the boil, add the mussels, cover with a tight fitting lid and cook over a medium heat, shaking the pan occasionally, for about 5 minutes until the mussels have opened. Discard any that haven't opened.

Scoop out the mussels using a slotted spoon, and place in individual serving bowls; cover and keep warm. Bring the cooking liquid back to the boil, and cook for 5 minutes to reduce down slightly. Stir in the parsley and cream, and adjust the seasoning if necessary. Ladle over the mussels and serve immediately with either crusty bread or chips, and a crisp salad.

Mustardy vegetable croustades

You can use any firm vegetable that will grate to make up this vegetarian supper dish. Kohlrabi is an autumnal tuber which grows above ground. The skin can be green to purple. Inside the flesh is pale and crisp with a mild radish/turnip-like flavour. It's great for stir-frying.

Serves 4

For the bases:
100 g (3½ oz) unsalted cashews, ground
100 g (3½ oz) vegetarian Cheddar cheese, grated
100 g (3½ oz) fresh white breadcrumbs
1 tbsp freshly chopped sage
1 garlic, clove, peeled and crushed
1 tbsp wholegrain mustard
50 g (2 oz) butter, melted
Salt and freshly ground black pepper

For the topping:
25 g (1 oz) butter
225 g (8 oz) leeks, trimmed, washed and finely shredded
225 g (8 oz) kohlrabi, peeled and grated
225 g (8 oz) celeriac
115 g (4 oz) carrot, peeled and grated
75 ml (3 fl oz) vegetable stock
1 tbsp wholegrain mustard
2 tbsp freshly chopped chives

Preheat the oven to 190°C (375°F, gas 5). First make the bases. Mix all the ingredients together and season well. Arrange 4 lightly greased 8.5 cm (3½ in) round x 2.5 cm (1 in) deep flan rings on a baking tray lined with baking parchment and press the mixture evenly into each to three quarters fill. Bake in the oven for about 25 minutes until golden. Carefully remove from the rings and keep warm.

Meanwhile, make the topping. Melt the butter in a frying pan until bubbling and stir fry the leeks, kohlrabi, celeriac and carrot for about 5 minutes. Add the stock, cover and simmer for a further 5 minutes until tender. Keep half the mixture warm and transfer the remaining mixture to a blender. Add the mustard and seasoning, and blend for a few seconds until smooth.

Smooth the puréed vegetables on top of the bases and pile the reserved vegetables on top. Sprinkle with chopped chives and serve immediately.

Stir-fried winter greens with bacon and chestnuts

For a change this year, why not serve this dish as a different Christmas Day roast accompaniment. Lots of lovely Winter ingredients which can all be prepared in advance and then quickly cooked at the last minute.

Serves 4

350 g (12 oz) Brussels sprouts
1 medium leek
225 g (8 oz) kale
1 tbsp vegetable oil
175 g (6 oz) smoked streaky bacon, chopped
2 tbsp Worcestershire sauce
115 g (4 oz) cooked, peeled chestnuts, chopped
2 tbsp freshly squeezed orange juice
½ tsp finely grated orange rind
Salt and freshly ground black pepper

Trim the Brussels sprouts and shred them finely. Trim the leek and cut in half lengthwise. Rinse under cold running water to flush out any trapped earth. Shake to remove excess water and then slice very thinly. Set aside.

Cut the curly kale leaves from the central stalks and chop roughly. Wash thoroughly and place in a saucepan without drying so that the kale will cook in the steam produced by the wet leaves. Cover and cook over a gentle heat for 10–12 minutes until tender. Drain well.

Meanwhile, heat the oil in a wok or large frying pan and stir fry the bacon for 2–3 minutes, then add the leek and shredded Brussels and cabbage continue to cook for a further minute.

Add the Worcestershire sauce and stir fry over a high heat for 3–4 minutes until just tender. Stir in the cooked kale and chestnuts and reheat for 1–2 minutes, then remove from the heat, and stir in the orange juice and rind, and season to taste. Serve immediately.

Tip: To prepare fresh chestnuts, put the chestnuts on a board, flat-side down, and using a pointed sharp knife, score the brown skin from the pointed end of the nut. Put in a pan of boiling water and cook for 10–20 minutes until the cuts open up. Drain and rinse in cold water, then carefully strips off the skins using a small pointed knife.

Celeriac gratin

A very knobbly skinned root with a surprisingly mild celery-like flavour and good firm texture. This is a very simple dish that goes very well with fish and poultry. Try not to over season to enjoy its flavour to best advantage.

Serves 4

900 g (2 lb) celeriac roots
Juice of 1 lemon
Salt and freshly ground black pepper
75 g (3 oz) butter
40 g (1½ oz) plain flour
300 ml (10 fl oz) whole milk
4 tbsp double cream
50 g (2 oz) freshly white breadcrumbs
50 g (2 oz) blanched almonds, finely chopped
1 tbsp fennel seeds

Preheat the oven to 190°C (375°F, gas 5). Peel the celeriac and cut into thin slices. Put in a large saucepan and toss in the lemon juice. Cover with water, add a good pinch of salt, bring to the boil and simmer for 6–7 minutes until just beginning to soften. Drain well, reserving 300 ml (10 fl oz) cooking liquid. Arrange the celeriac in an ovenproof gratin dish.

Meanwhile, melt 40 g (1½ oz) butter in a saucepan and add the flour; cook, stirring for 1 minute. Remove from the heat and gradually stir in the milk, cream and reserved cooking liquid. Season well. Return to the heat and gradually bring to the boil, stirring, and cook for 1 minute until thickened. Pour the sauce over the celeriac and stand the dish on a baking tray.

Mix the remaining ingredients together and sprinkle over the celeriac. Dot with remaining butter and bake in the oven for 35–40 minutes until golden and crisp. Serve immediately.

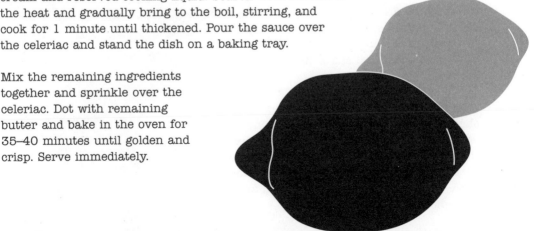

Perfect roast roots

I couldn't let the opportunity pass me by and not include a recipe for everyone's favourite roast dinner veggies. Here I'm keeping with tradition and using potatoes, parsnips and carrots. Choose same-sized veggies for even cooking results.

Serves 6–8

900 g (2 lb) medium-sized roasting potatoes such as Maris Piper or Rooster
350 g (12 oz) small, same size carrots, peeled
Salt
350 g (12 oz) small, same size parsnips, peeled
2 tbsp plain flour
Freshly ground black pepper
1 tsp coriander seeds, crushed
1 tsp mustard seeds, crushed
115 g (4 oz) goose fat, beef dripping or lard, or 6 tbsp cold pressed rapeseed oil

Preheat the oven to 200°C (400°F, gas 6). Peel the potatoes thinly and cut into even-sized pieces (you can leave smaller ones whole).

Place the potatoes in a saucepan with the carrots and barely cover with cold water. Add a pinch of salt and bring to the boil. Add the parsnips, bring back to the boil and cook, uncovered, for 5 minutes. Drain well and allow to dry in the colander or sieve for about 10 minutes. Return to the saucepan, cover, and then shake the pan to 'rough up' the edges of the potatoes. Carefully mix in the flour, pepper and spices to give a light coating.

Heat the goose fat, dripping, lard or oil in a shallow sided roasting tin for 3–4 minutes until very hot and carefully add the vegetables, tossing them in the hot fat to coat. Bake in the oven for about 40–50 minutes, turning occasionally, until golden and crisp all over. Drain and serve immediately.

Creamy Jerusalem artichoke and potato bake

A version of the classic 'dauphinoise' potato dish which packs a punch on the taste buds and makes a good accompaniment for steaks, game dishes and rich meaty stews.

Serves 4

75 g (3 oz) lightly salted butter, softened
1 lemon
350 g (12 oz) Jerusalem artichokes
350 g (12 oz) medium-sized waxy textured potatoes, such as Charlotte potatoes
150 ml (5 fl oz) milk
150 ml (5 fl oz) double cream
1 garlic clove, peeled and crushed
Salt and freshly ground black pepper
2 tbsp freshly chopped parsley

Preheat the oven to 170°C (325°F, gas 3). Grease the inside of a 1.2 l (2 pt) gratin dish with half the butter.

Cut the lemon in half and squeeze the juice into a large bowl. Half fill with cold water. Peel the artichokes, putting them in the lemony water as you go, and then slice them thinly, placing back in the lemony water until required.

Peel the potatoes and slice thinly – the thinner you cut them, the quicker the gratin will cook. Drain the Jerusalem artichokes well, and pat dry with kitchen paper. Lay them neatly inside the prepared dish and top with the potato slices.

Mix the milk, cream and garlic together and season well. Pour over the sliced vegetables. Dot with remaining butter. Stand the gratin dish on a baking sheet and bake in the oven for about 1½ hours or until very tender. Serve sprinkled with black pepper and chopped parsley.

Sweet onion and cheesy bread

This is one of my favourite recipes in the book. A big hunk of this with a hearty soup makes a filling meal, but it's equally good sliced and served with cheese and chutney.

Serves 12

50 g (2 oz) butter
450 g (1 lb) onions, peeled and chopped
1 tbsp caster sugar
500 g (1 lb 2 oz) strong white bread flour
1 tsp salt
2 tsp instant or fast-acting dried yeast
150 g (5 oz) mature locally produced Cheddar-type cheese, grated
Approx. 300 ml (10 fl oz) lukewarm water
1 free range egg, beaten

Melt the butter in a large frying pan until bubbling and fry the onions for 5 minutes until softened but not browned. Reduce the heat, cover and cook gently for about 30 minutes, stirring occasionally, until very tender. Stir in the sugar, raise the heat and cook, stirring, for 8–10 minutes until golden and caramelised – take care not to burn. Set aside to cool.

Sieve the flour and salt into a bowl and stir in the dried yeast and 115 g (4 oz) cheese. Make a well in the centre and add the oniony butter mixture and sufficient water to bring together to form a firm mixture.

Turn the dough on to a lightly floured surface and knead for about 5 minutes to form a smooth, round ball. Put in a flour dusted bowl, cover loosely and stand in a warm place for about an hour until double the size.

Once the dough has risen, re-knead and form into an approx. 19 cm (7 in) round; lightly cover with a piece of oiled clear wrap and leave in a warm place for about 1 hour until doubled in size. Preheat the oven to 220°C (425°F, gas 7).

Brush the top of the dough with egg and sprinkle with remaining cheese. Bake in the oven for about 25 minutes until richly golden and hollow sounding when tapped. Transfer to a wire rack to cool. Best served warm.

Curried parsnip bhajis

This familiar sweet root vegetable lends itself so well to Indian spices that I decided not to do anything too contemporary with the flavourings. You can enjoy this recipe as a snack, starter or part of a main meal curry.

Makes 12

25 g (1 oz) butter
1 garlic clove, peeled and crushed
2 shallots, peeled and finely chopped
1 tsp Madras curry paste
450 g (1 lb) cold cooked parsnip, mashed
6 tbsp gram (chickpea) flour
4 tbsp freshly chopped coriander
Salt and freshly ground black pepper
Sunflower oil for deep-frying

For the dip:
150 ml (5 fl oz) whole milk yogurt
2 tbsp spicy mango chutney
2 tbsp freshly chopped mint or coriander

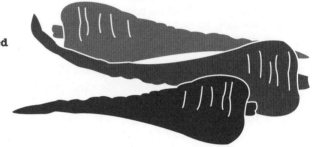

Melt the butter in a small frying pan until bubbling and then gently fry the garlic and shallots for 5 minutes until softened but not brown. Stir in the curry paste and set aside to cool.

Put the mashed parsnip in a bowl and add the coriander and plenty of seasoning, and mix together with the cold curried garlic and shallot butter. Stir in 4 Tbsp gram flour to form a stiff mixture. Cover and chill for 30 minutes.

Divide the parsnip mixture into 12 equal portions and form each into a ball, dusting with flour to prevent sticking. Place on a baking parchment lined board and flatten slightly to a thickness of 2 cm (¾ in).

Heat the oil for deep-frying to 190°C (375°F). Cook the bhajis in 3 batches for about 5 minutes until crisp and richly golden. Drain well and keep warm whilst frying each batch.

Mix up the dip ingredients and serve immediately with the warm bhajis.

Cinnamon toast and buttered apples

Some of life's simple pleasures are often food related, and here's one of mine. Toasted buttery bread with sweet spice and honey and tender, juicy apples to accompany. Mmmm!

Serves 4

75 g (3 oz) butter
1 tsp ground cinnamon plus extra to dust
3 tbsp clear local honey
4 thick slices white bread, crusts removed
4 eating apples, peeled, cored and cut into thick slices
Juice of 1 lemon

Melt 50 g (2 oz) butter in a small saucepan, add 1 tsp cinnamon and 1 tbsp honey. Preheat the grill to a hot setting and toast the bread lightly on both sides. Remove from the grill and brush the buttery syrup on one side. Return to the grill and cook for a few seconds longer until the toast is golden and bubbling. Set aside and keep warm.

Toss the apple rings in the lemon juice. Melt the remaining butter in a frying pan until bubbling. Drain the apples and stir fry them for 4–5 minutes until tender. Pile the apples on top of the toast and serve warm, dusted with more cinnamon and a dollop of whipped cream or yogurt.

Roast pears with whisky and oat cream

This is an easy pudding with lots of Scottish flavours, which is just the ticket to warm you up on a Winter's evening.

4 ripe pears
Juice of 1 lemon
2 tbsp well flavoured local honey
50 g (2 oz) unsalted butter

For the oat cream:
2 tbsp fine oatmeal
200 ml (7 fl oz) double cream
2–3 tbsp whisky
1 tbsp well flavoured local honey, such as heather

Preheat the oven to 200°C (400°F, gas 6). Peel and halve the pears. Place in a shallow roasting tin and toss in the lemon juice. In a small saucepan, gently melt the honey and butter together, and then drizzle over the pears. Bake for about 30 minutes until tender, basting occasionally.

Meanwhile, make the oaty cream. Sprinkle the oatmeal evenly over the bottom of a small heavy based frying pan and heat over a medium heat, stirring, for 2–3 minutes until lightly toasted – take care not to burn. Allow to cool.

When the oatmeal is cold, whip the cream until just peaking and fold in whisky to taste, oatmeal and honey. Serve with the warm pears.

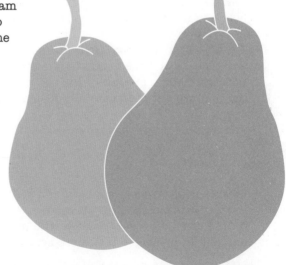

Chocolate chestnut cake with coffee icing

I associate chestnuts mostly with French cooking where they are often used in rich creamy desserts. I thought I'd have a go at incorporating them in a cake, and the result is a dense, rich bake, full of flavour and moist texture.

Serves 8–10

115 g (4 oz) good quality 85% cocoa dark chocolate
225 g (8 oz) light brown sugar
115 g (4 oz) unsalted butter, softened
5 free range eggs, separated
3 tbsp brandy
100 g (3½ oz) ground almonds
450 g (1 lb) peeled chestnuts, ground (see page 132 for preparation)

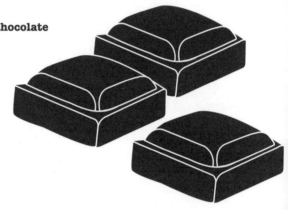

For the icing:
250 g (9 oz) icing sugar
1 tbsp liquid coffee
5 tsp warm water

A few marrons glacés or grated plain chocolate to decorate

Preheat the oven to 180°C (350°F, gas 4). Grease and flour the sides and base-line a 23 cm (9 in) spring form round cake tin. Put the chocolate, sugar and butter in a saucepan and heat gently until melted together. Cool for 10 minutes.

Transfer to a heatproof bowl and mix in the egg yolks and brandy, and fold in the almonds and chestnuts. In a large, grease free bowl, whisk the egg whites until stiff. Mix a quarter of the egg white into the chocolate mixture to loosen the mixture and then carefully fold in the remainder.

Pile into the prepared cake tin, smooth off the top and bake in the oven for 45–50 minutes until risen and firm to the touch. Allow to cool in the tin, then transfer to a wire rack.

Sift the icing sugar into a bowl and gradually mix in the coffee and water to form a soft smooth icing. Spread over the top of the cake, allowing the icing to drizzle down the side. Decorate with marrons glacés or grated chocolate, if liked, and allow the icing to set before serving.

Tip: Try serving warm, uniced, with coffee ice cream!

Carrot and ginger pudding

I've been adding grated carrot to cake mixtures for quite a while now, even my Christmas pudding recipe, because it gives a natural sweetness and added moistness. This is a steamed pudding which could make a lighter alternative to the traditional richer Christmas puddings.

Serves 8

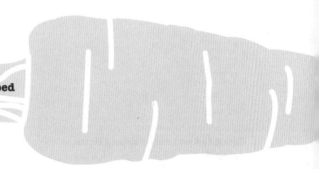

175 g (6 oz) unsalted butter
175 g (6 oz) light brown sugar
3 free range eggs, beaten
25 g (1 oz) preserved ginger, finely chopped
50 g (2 oz) sultanas
75 g (3 oz) grated carrot
175 g (6 oz) self raising flour
1 tsp ground ginger
½ tsp salt

1 quantity Crème anglaise (see page 171), to serve

Grease a 1.2 l (40 fl oz) pudding basin and place a small disc of baking parchment in the bottom.

In a bowl cream together the butter and sugar together until paler, thick and creamy. Gradually whisk in the eggs and stir in the chopped ginger, sultanas and grated carrot.

Sift the flour, ground ginger and salt into the bowl and carefully fold into the carrot and ginger mixture. Spoon into the prepared basin and smooth the top. Top the pudding with a round of baking parchment, and then cover the top of the pudding basin with a layer of pleated foil. Secure with string.

Half fill a large saucepan with water and bring to the boil. Either place the pudding in a steamer compartment over the saucepan or stand on a trivet in the saucepan. Cover tightly with a lid and steam for about 2½ hours, topping the water level up as required, until the pudding is risen and firm to the touch – a skewer inserted into the centre of the pudding should come out clean.

To serve, unwrap the pudding and invert on to a warmed serving plate. Serve at once with crème anglaise.

Rhubarb and tangerine dumpling

It's a good reminder that Spring is on its way when you see the bright pink stems appear in the shops for the first time. This is an old fashioned pudding based on a classic, Sussex Pond Pudding, from the part of the country where I grew up.

Serves 6–8

350 g (12 oz) self-raising flour
½ tsp salt
175 g (6 oz) suet
Approx. 225 ml (8 fl oz) water
450 g (1 lb) rhubarb, trimmed and cut into 2 cm (¾ in) pieces
115 g (4 oz) light brown sugar
1 tangerine
½ tsp ground allspice

Grease a 1.2 l (40 fl oz) pudding basin and place a small disc of baking parchment in the bottom.

Place the flour and salt in a bowl and mix in the suet along with sufficient water to make a light, elastic dough. Roll out two thirds of the dough on a lightly floured surface, 2.5 cm (1 in) larger all round than the top of the prepared basin and carefully ease the pastry into the basin to line it.

In a bowl, mix the rhubarb and sugar together. Carefully grate the rind from the tangerine, then peel and roughly chop the flesh. Add the rind and flesh to the rhubarb along with the allspice and mix well. Pack into the lined basin.

Roll out the remaining pastry to form a circle to fit the top of the basin. Dampen the edge with water and seal on the pastry lid. Top the pudding with a round of baking parchment, and then cover the top of the pudding basin with a layer of pleated foil. Secure with string.

Half fill a large saucepan with water and bring to the boil. Either place the pudding in a steamer compartment over the saucepan or stand on a trivet in the saucepan. Cover tightly with a lid and steam for about 2½ hours, topping the water level up as required, until the pudding is risen and firm to the touch – insert a skewer into the centre of the pudding to make sure the rhubarb is tender.

To serve, unwrap the pudding and invert on to a warmed serving plate with a lipped edge – the pudding will be very juicy when it is cut. Serve at once with vanilla ice cream.

Honeyed hazelnut tart

This is my British version of the American favourite pecan pie. Hazel nuts have a sweeter flavour than most other nuts and lend themselves well to honey. If you prefer a more savoury nut, then try walnut halves. I think the tart is best served warm with whipped cream, although when cold it goes well with a mid morning cup of coffee!

Serves 8

300 g (10 oz) readymade sweet
    shortcrust pastry
25 g (1 oz) unsalted butter, melted
50 g (2 oz) caster sugar
1½ tsp cornflour
Pinch of salt
75 ml (3 fl oz) well flavoured local honey,
    such as heather
75 ml (3 fl oz) golden syrup
2 free range eggs, beaten
200 g (7 oz) hazelnuts, lightly crushed

Preheat the oven to 180°C (350°F, gas 4). On a lightly floured surface roll out the pastry to fit a 23-cm (9-in) loose-bottomed flan tin. Trim and chill until required.

Meanwhile, make the filling. In a large jug, whisk together the remaining ingredients, except the hazelnuts.

Arrange the hazelnuts neatly in the pastry case and stand the tin on a baking sheet. Pour over the filling and bake in the oven for about 50 minutes until set. Leave to cool in the tin for 20 minutes, then carefully transfer to a serving plate. Best served warm whipped cream.

I really enjoy making my own jams and chutneys. Much like making bread and baking, I find it therapeutic and relaxing. I also find the results very rewarding and unable to be matched by anything you can buy in the shops. Homemade preserves are also greatly appreciated as presents.

PRESERVES

& Accompaniments

Home preserving is the best way to capture the flavours of the seasons for all year round enjoyment. Preserving means you can make the most of a glut of food, especially if you grow your own, or have access to a pick-your-own farm or orchard. If you look around you at the right time of the year you'll see lots of free, wild foods that you can preserve and keep too – anything you haven't had to pay for always tastes better in my opinion!

In this chapter you'll find notes on basic freezing techniques – probably the easiest way to store food successfully – and tips on jam and chutney making. I have included recipes to cover other techniques such as pickling, chutney making and syruping – all good ways of enjoying foods out of season. So whether you want a recipe for a simple jam or something more involved, you should find something to suit, and once you've mastered the basics, you'll soon see how easy it is to make the most of just about every food by preserving it in some way.

There are also basic recipes for accompaniments, sauces and dressings to go with the other recipes in the book, to enable you to add the perfect finish to your dish.

General tips for freezing fruit and vegetables

Without doubt, freezing is the best way to preserve fruit and vegetables and it means that you can enjoy your locally grown produce out of season, when there is limited choice of fresh. Most fruit and vegetables will keep for up to 12 months in the freezer giving you year round enjoyment – particularly good if you have a glut of produce. Choose only top quality, ripe, fresh produce for freezing – although slightly over-ripe fruit can be frozen in purée form.

Preparation – wash unpeeled fruit and vegetables well and remove leaves and stalks as necessary.

Blanching – the process by which vegetables are plunged into boiling water and, after the water comes back to boiling, are boiled for a short period of time. This inactivates enzymes which would otherwise make the food deteriorate, and helps to retain vitamin C. Once the recommended boiling period is up – usually between 1 and 3 minutes, plunge the vegetables into iced water to cool as soon as possible, or place under running cold water. Pat dry thoroughly using kitchen paper in order to prevent too much ice forming during freezing and individual pieces sticking together in a solid lump.

Open freezing – particularly good for berries or prepared pieces of fruit and vegetable. Lay on trays lined with baking parchment and place in the freezer until solid. Either seal in freezer bags trying to expel as much air out of the bag as possible, or pack in rigid containers with fitted lids. Label and store until required. Freezing produce in this way will enable you to take out small measures from the bag at a time because the fruit shouldn't stick together once frozen and packed.

Purée and cooked – raw, ripe fruit such as berries and peaches can be puréed and packed into small rigid containers to freeze. If smaller quantities are required, freeze in ice cube trays and then transfer to freezer bags – you can then defrost small amounts as necessary. Fruit purée that discolours such as peaches should be mixed with a little lemon juice or sugar to prevent browning. Purée is excellent for making sauces for ice cream, fruit coulis, and fruit fools. Cooked fruit can also be puréed down and frozen in the same way – stewed apples, plums and compotes freeze well in a purée.

Freezing fruit in sugar – use approx. 75–115 g (3–4 oz) caster sugar per 450 g (1 lb) fruit depending on how sweet the fruit is. As you layer the prepared fruit in its container, sprinkle lightly with sugar. On defrosting, the sugar will make its own juice. This is a good way to preserve a mixture of berries as once they defrost you have a readymade compote or topping for a cheesecake.

Freezing fruit in sugar syrup – some fruits discolour easily for example peaches and apricots, and so a sugar syrup with added lemon juice is useful in order to prevent this. Dissolve 450 g (1 lb) caster sugar in 600 ml (20 fl oz) water and allow to cool completely. Stir in 2 tbsp lemon juice. Pack the prepared fruit into rigid freezer containers and pour over the syrup. Place a piece of baking parchment directly on top of the fruit in order to keep the fruit pieces submerged before you put the lid on. Label and store until required.

Basic techniques for jam and chutney making

Choosing and preparation – it is essential that you start with the best quality produce in order to prevent rapid deterioration during storage. Fruit and vegetables should be slightly under ripe or perfectly ripe depending on the recipe; blemish free, and especially free from mould and mildew. It should be correctly prepared.

Cooking fruit – prepared fruit is often simmered either on its own or with liquid before sugar is added. Cook the fruit slowly, without covering (unless otherwise stated), stirring occasionally until just softened. This will allow you to obtain the maximum amount of juice from the fruit. If there is a lack of juice, add a bit more water – this might occur if the fruit is firmer than usual. Take care not to overcook the fruit at this stage otherwise flavour and colour will be impaired.

Testing for setting point for jams, jellies, marmalade, conserves and fruit cheese – there are 2 main ways that I use to find out if a preserve has reached the right point in order to set:

Using a sugar thermometer – for jam, marmalade, conserves and fruit cheese, an acceptable reading range is from 104–105.5°C (219–222°F). The lower temperature will give a softer set than the higher one – used for conserves. Use the higher temperature for fruit cheeses. For jellies, use 104–105°C (219–221°F).

The wrinkle test – take the saucepan of boiling preserve off the heat and quickly spoon a little preserve on to a cold flat plate; allow to cool. If the preserve is ready, a slight skin will form on the spoonful and will wrinkle when pushed with your finger. Return the saucepan to the boil if the preserve isn't ready and retest after about 2 minutes further boiling.

Preparing storage jars and bottles – use sound glass containers and bottles with no chips or cracks. Wash thoroughly in very hot water with mild detergent, and rinse well. To sterilise jars and bottles, put them open side up in a deep saucepan, cover with boiling water and boil for 10 minutes. Carefully lift out with tongs and leave to drain upside down on a thick clean towel. Dry with a clean cloth if necessary and place on a baking tray lined with a few layers of kitchen paper; keep warm in the oven on the lowest setting until ready to fill.

Filling the jars – a clean ladle or small heatproof jug will be useful to help you transfer the preserve to the prepared jar or bottle. If the preserve is very fruity or contains rind and small pieces, stir well before putting in the jars. Fill to within 6 mm (¼ in) of the top of the jar. Half filled jars of preserve should be cooled, sealed and kept in the fridge and eaten as soon as possible.

Sealing – to prevent spoiling during storage it is essential to achieve an airtight seal on your preserves. As soon as the preserve is in the jars, place a waxed paper circle directly on the top of the jam – available in packs with jam pot covers. Either top with a screw-on lid or seal tightly with the transparent jam pot covers and an elastic band. If you have lots of jars to fill, it is better to allow the preserve to cool completely in the jars before sealing with waxed paper circles and lids. Avoid covering semi-cold preserves as too much condensation will form and this could encourage mould to grow during storage. For chutneys, pickles and other preserves with vinegar, make sure the seals used are non-corrosive.

Storage – don't forget to label your preserve jars and bottles with its contents and date it was made. Keep in a cool, dry, dark place in order to preserve colour and quality. If perfectly prepared and stored, most jams and jellies will keep for up to 12 months; chutneys, pickles and vinegars for around 6–8 months, and fruit cheeses up to 6 months. See specific recipes for other storage instructions.

Lavender vinegar

Choose to pick lavender just as the buds have swollen and are about to break into flower. If white balsamic vinegar is unavailable, choose white wine or sherry vinegar for best results.

Makes 500 ml (17 fl oz)

A few sprigs fresh lavender
500 ml (17 fl oz) white balsamic vinegar

Wash and pat dry the lavender sprigs using absorbent kitchen paper. Line a board with clear wrap and arrange the lavender on top. Lay a sheet of greaseproof paper on top and gently crush using a rolling pin to allow the flavour to be extracted. Push into sterilised bottles.

Lightly warm the vinegar (but do not allow to get hot) and pour over the lavender to fill the bottle. Seal with a non-corrosive, acid-proof lid. Set on a sunny windowsill and shake daily for about 2 weeks. Test for flavour and either store as it is (remembering the flavour will get stronger) or strain and rebottle. For a much stronger flavour, strain and rebottle with more fresh lavender.

Note: This is the same method to use with other fresh herbs such as basil, fennel, lemon balm, marjoram, rosemary, sage, tarragon and thyme.

Herb and garlic oil

The oil you choose is up to personal preference. I like to use a mild oil such as sunflower or safflower so that the flavour of the herbs really comes through. For a stronger taste, choose a more flavoured cold pressed rapeseed oil or even a nut oil such as walnut.

Makes 600 ml (20 fl oz)

2 sprigs fresh thyme
2 sprigs fresh rosemary
2 bay leaves
3 cloves garlic, unpeeled
600 ml (20 fl oz) light flavoured oil such as, safflower or sunflower oil

Wash and pat dry the herbs using absorbent kitchen paper. Push into sterilised bottles.

Lightly warm the oil (but do not allow to get hot) and pour over the herbs and garlic to fill the bottle. Seal with a non-corrosive lid. Set on a sunny windowsill and shake daily for about 2 weeks. Test for flavour and either store as it is (remembering the flavour will get stronger) or strain and rebottle. For a much stronger flavour, strain and rebottle with more fresh herbs and garlic.

Mint sauce

Apple sauce

A classic accompaniment to roast lamb, but also a good flavouring for yogurt dips, sauces and salad dressings. Spearmint is the traditional mint used in this recipe – it is commonly available and has a sweeter mint flavour.

A traditional accompaniment to roast pork, goose or duck, but this sweet, smooth purée makes a lovely a fruity base for a pie or tart or as a filling with whipped cream in a sponge cake.

Serves 6–8

3 tbsp freshly chopped spearmint
1½ tbsp caster sugar
2 tbsp boiling water
150 ml (5 fl oz) white wine or clear malt
    vinegar

In a non reactive bowl, mix the mint with the caster sugar. Add the boiling water and stir until the sugar dissolves. Set aside to cool.

Stir in the vinegar and stand for 30 minutes before serving. To store, pour into a clean glass jar and seal tightly with a non-corrosive, acid-proof lid. Keep in the fridge for up to a week.

Serves 6–8 as an accompaniment

500 g (1 lb 2 oz) cooking apples with a
    floury texture such as Bramley
2 tbsp freshly squeezed lemon juice
25 g (1 oz) unsalted butter
3–4 tbsp caster sugar

Peel, core and chop the apples. Place in a saucepan and toss in the lemon juice. Heat gently until steaming, then cover and simmer gently for about 5 minutes until soft and collapsed. Remove from the heat and beat with a wooden spoon until smooth – for an ultra-smooth texture, push through a nylon sieve. Stir in the butter, and add sugar to taste. Serve hot or cold.

Redcurrant jelly

A beautiful claret coloured preserve that can be enjoyed as a sweet spread or more traditionally as an accompaniment to rich meats like lamb or game. Use the same method with blackcurrants and white currants.

Makes approx. 675 g (1½ lb)

**1 kg (2 lb 3½ oz) just ripe redcurrants, washed
approx. 350 g (12 oz) granulated sugar per 450 ml (15 fl oz) juice**

Using a fork, run it down the length of each branch of currants to remove the stems. Place the redcurrants in a preserving pan or large saucepan and pour over 150 ml (5 fl oz) water. Bring to the boil and simmer for about 5 minutes until very tender, crushing them whilst they cook.

Strain the fruit and its juices through a jelly bag or some clean muslin suspended over a clean bowl – this will take at least 6 hours to allow the fruit left behind to become dry – don't be tempted to squeeze the mixture otherwise the finished preserve will be cloudy.

Measure the juice and pour back into the saucepan. Add 350 g (12 oz) sugar per 450 ml (15 fl oz) juice. Heat, stirring over a low heat until the sugar is dissolved. Raise the heat and boil rapidly for 8–10 minutes or until setting point is reached – see page 149. Skim off any surface foam using a flat spoon. Pour into hot jars and seal as described on page 149.

Note: If the redcurrants are very ripe, you will not need to add any water to the mixture at the beginning.

Mayonnaise

Perfect gravy

Often thought of as difficult to make, nothing beats the flavour of a homemade mayonnaise with fresh seafood. It is essential to allow plenty of time because you really must add the oil gradually – it just can't be rushed.

Homemade gravy is so much nicer than the ready made, convenience types. Simply change the flavourings depending on whether you're cooking beef, lamb, pork or poultry.

Serves 6

Makes approx. 200 ml (7 fl oz)

1 medium organic egg yolk
¼ tsp dry mustard powder
¼ tsp salt
Pinch of ground white pepper
¼ tsp caster sugar
approx. 150 ml (5 fl oz) light flavoured oil such as sunflower oil
1 tbsp white wine vinegar

2 tbsp plain flour
4 tbsp reserved meat cooking juices
600 ml (20 fl oz) fresh meat stock (see page 156)
Few drops gravy browning (optional)
Salt and freshly ground black pepper

Place the egg yolk in a bowl with the mustard, salt, pepper and sugar. Mix well. Add the oil, drop by drop, whisking until thick, smooth and glossy. When sufficient oil has been added, carefully fold in the vinegar and mix thoroughly. Cover and chill until required.

Blend the flour with the reserved cooking juices in a saucepan, and gradually stir in the beef stock. Bring to the boil, stirring, and simmer for 3 minutes, until thickened. Add gravy browning, if using, and season well before serving.

Note: If the mixture 'splits' or curdles, put another egg yolk in a basin and gradually add the split mixture as above.

Note: If you want to add your accompanying vegetable cooking water to the gravy, replace the stock with an equal amount of the water – you'll end up with a less meaty, more fragrant gravy.

Creamed horseradish relish

Horseradish needs to be used as soon as it's prepared in order to make the most of its famously pungent flesh. It is used raw because the flavour is lost on cooking.

Serves 4

40 g (1½ oz) piece horseradish root
6 tbsp soured cream
1 tsp Dijon mustard
2 tsp white wine vinegar
1 tsp caster sugar
Salt and freshly ground black pepper

Peel and finely grate or mince the horseradish – see note below. Place in a small bowl and mix with the remaining ingredients, and fold into the cream. Serve with hot or cold roast beef, cold smoked ham, or smoked fish.

Note: Horseradish is very pungent, when peeled and prepared, so handle with care. The easiest (and most comfortable) way to grate it is to use a food processor. It will go brown is prepared in advance, but can be grated and frozen in sealed bags or containers for up to 6 months.

Homemade stock

To make the most of the flavour of fresh local produce, it is worth making your own stock if you have the time. For meat and poultry, the method is exactly the same, but you may want to add less or increase the flavourings depending on how flavoursome you want your stock to be.

Makes approx. 1.2 l (40 fl oz)

900 g (2 lb) meat bones or chicken carcass, fresh or from cooked meat
2 celery sticks, trimmed and diced
1 large onion, peeled and quartered
1 large carrot, scrubbed and diced
Few sprigs fresh parsley
Few sprigs fresh thyme
1–2 bay leaves
Salt and freshly ground black pepper
2 l (67 fl oz) cold water

Wash the bones if fresh, and then chop them roughly or break down the carcass and bones of the chicken. Place the bones in a large saucepan along with the other ingredients. Pour over the water and bring to the boil. Skim away the surface scum using a flat spoon, reduce the heat to a very gentle simmer, partially cover and cook for about 3 hours. Remove from the heat and allow to cool.

Line a sieve with muslin and place over a large jug or bowl. Strain the stock and store, covered, in the fridge for up to 3 days. Skim away any surface fat before using. Alternatively, freeze in small batches.

Note: For a vegetable stock, follow the recipe above omitting the meat, and doubling the vegetable quantity. Add the same quantity of water and cook as above for 45 minutes. Cool, strain and store as above. Makes about 1.5 l (50 fl oz) stock. For a fish stock, follow the recipe for meat stock, replacing the meat with 900 g (2 lb) white fish trimmings (skin, head, bone and scraps). Add the same quantity of water and cook as above for 30 minutes. Cool, strain and store as above. Makes about 1.5 l (50 fl oz) stock.

Fresh tomato sauce

This classic Italian-style tomato sauce can be used as a base for many recipes likes soups, casseroles, pizzas or pasta dishes. Any herbs can be used in this recipe according to preference.

Makes approx. 600 ml (20 fl oz)

1.25 kg (2 lb 12 oz) ripe plum or tasty tomatoes, washed and halved
Large sprig each of rosemary, thyme and oregano
1 bay leaf
2 garlic cloves, peeled, left whole
1 tsp caster sugar
½ tsp salt
50 g (2 oz) unsalted butter
2 tbsp cold pressed rapeseed oil

Place the tomato halves in the bottom of a large saucepan or frying pan with a lid. Tie the herbs and bay leaf together and place on top of the tomatoes. Add the garlic cloves and cover with a lid. Cook over a low/medium heat for about 40 minutes until soft and collapsed – keep the heat quite low to prevent burning.

Discard the herbs and push the pulpy tomato mixture through a nylon sieve to form a thick juice, leaving a dry residue of skins and seeds in the sieve. Return to a clean saucepan and add the remaining ingredients. Heat gently until the butter melts, then simmer gently for about 35 minutes until thickened, but still thin enough to pour. Use as per recipe or allow to cool, cover and store in the fridge until required for a maximum of 3 days. To freeze, ladle into small containers when cool, seal and freeze for up to 6 months. Thaw in the fridge overnight.

Bramble (blackberry) jelly

One of my favourite preserves. It reminds me of the end of the school Summer holidays when we used to go bramble picking in the nearby fields. Sadly those fields are long gone, but my love for the rich flavour remains.

Makes approx. 750 g (1 lb 10 oz)

1 kg (2 lb 3½ oz) blackberries, washed and hulled
Approx. 500 g (1 lb 2 oz) preserving sugar
Approx. 2 tbsp freshly squeezed lemon juice

Place in a large saucepan or preserving pan and add 150 ml (5 fl oz) water. Bring to the boil and simmer for 10 minutes until very soft, pressing the fruit occasionally.

Strain the fruit and its juices through a jelly bag or some clean muslin suspended over a clean bowl – this will take about 6 hours to allow the fruit left behind to become dry – don't be tempted to squeeze the mixture.

Measure the juice and pour back into the saucepan. Add 500 g (1 lb 2 oz) sugar and 2 tbsp lemon juice per 600 ml (20 fl oz) blackberry juice. Heat, stirring over a low heat until the sugar is dissolved. Raise the heat and boil rapidly for about 15 minutes until setting point is reached – see page 149. Skim off any surface foam using a flat spoon. Pour into hot jars and seal as described on page 149.

Blueberry jam

Another one of my favourite preserves. It's delicious spooned over pancakes, ice cream and freshly baked scones. If the blueberries aren't particularly ripe, add about 5 tbsp water to the blueberries when simmering.

Makes approx. 600 g (1 lb 5 oz)

450 g (1 lb) ripe blueberries or blaeberries (bilberries), stalks removed, washed
450 g (1 lb) granulated sugar

Place the blueberries in a saucepan over a gentle heat, stirring until the juice flows. Once soft, stir in the sugar. Continue to stir over a low heat until the sugar dissolves, then stir in the blueberries. Raise the heat and boil rapidly until setting point is reached – see page 149. Spoon into hot jars and seal as described on page 149.

Peach conserve

Not quite as good as eating a raw fresh peach, but peaches still make a worthy preserve. Its gloriously golden-orange colour is guaranteed to brighten up a cold Winter's day breakfast or tea. A conserve has more fruit pieces and a softer consistency than a traditional jam

Makes approx. 600 g (1 lb 5 oz)

450 g (1 lb) ripe yellow-fleshed peaches, skinned
450 g (1 lb) granulated sugar
2 tbsp lemon juice

Halve the peaches and remove the stones. Crack the stones using a rolling pin and tie them in a muslin bag. Chop the peaches finely and place in a non-corrosive bowl with the muslin bag. Mix in the sugar and lemon juice, and allow to stand for 15 minutes only, stirring occasionally, to allow the flavours to develop, but not allowing the fruit to discolour.

Transfer to a saucepan, and heat gently until the sugar dissolves, stirring all the time. Remove the stone bag, raise the heat and cook steadily until setting point is reached – see page 149. Allow to cool slightly, stir to distribute the fruit then discard the muslin bag, and spoon into hot jars and seal as described on page 149.

Note: Follow the quantities and method above using nectarines, greengages, plums, or apricots (it is not necessary to skin greengages, plums or apricots).

Gooseberry curd

Usually, fruit curds are made with citrus fruits, but this recipe works well with gooseberries, and also with cooking apples and apricots (but add 2 tablespoons lemon juice to the mixture).

Makes approx. 450 g (1 lb)

450 g (1 lb) cooking gooseberries
150 ml (5 fl oz) water
Approx. 50 g (2 oz) unsalted butter
Approx. 225 g (8 oz) caster sugar
Approx. 3 medium organic or free range egg yolks

Wash the gooseberries but there is no need to top and tail. Place in a saucepan with the water and bring to the boil. Simmer for 6–8 minutes until thick and pulpy. Push through a nylon sieve to form a smooth purée.

Measure the purée and place in a large heatproof bowl. Add 50 g (2 oz) butter and 225 g (8 oz) sugar per 300 ml (10 fl oz) purée. Stand the bowl over a saucepan of barely simmering water and cook, stirring, until the butter melts and the sugar dissolves. Add 3 egg yolks per 300 ml (10 fl oz) purée and cook, stirring, until sufficiently thick to cover the back of a wooden spoon – this will take approx. 25–30 minutes. Spoon into hot sterilised jars and seal as described on page 149. Allow to cool and store in the fridge for up to 1 month. Once opened, keep in the fridge and use within 1 week.

Pumpkin butter

Use this rich amber preserve like jam or as a filling for tarts and cakes. I like to add a little spice to the mix but it's up to personal taste. You can also use butternut squash flesh for this recipe.

Makes approx. 600 g (1 lb 5 oz)

450 g (1 lb) prepared pumpkin flesh – skin and seeds removed
1 tsp salt
Finely grated rind and juice 1 small lemon
450 g (1 lb) caster sugar
50 g (2 oz) unsalted butter
¼ tsp ground nutmeg

Cut the pumpkin flesh into small pieces and place in a steamer or colander. Sprinkle with the salt, cover and cook over boiling water for 30 minutes, turning occasionally, until tender. Transfer to a heatproof bowl and mash well using a potato masher.

Put the mash in a saucepan and stir in the lemon rind and juice, caster sugar and butter. Stir over a low heat until the sugar dissolves and the butter melts. Raise the heat, bring to the boil and simmer gently, stirring to prevent the mixture sticking on the bottom of the pan, for about 20 minutes until very thick. Add nutmeg. Spoon into hot sterilised jars and seal as described on page 149.

Allow to cool and store for up to 6 months.
Once opened, keep in the fridge
and use within 2 weeks.

Rowan and apple jelly

Depending on the part of the country you live, the rowan tree's bitter orangey-red berries ripen from late August onwards, just make sure you get them before the birds do! This is a firm set jelly and is a traditional accompaniment to rich meat and game dishes.

Makes approx. 675 g (1½ lb)

500 g (1 lb 2 oz) rowanberries, stripped from the stalks and well washed
500 g (1 lb 2 oz) cooking apples, cored, peeled and roughly chopped
650 ml (22 fl oz) water
375 g (13 oz) granulated sugar

Put the rowan berries and chopped apples in a large saucepan and pour over 450 ml (15 fl oz) water. Bring to the boil and simmer for 10–15 minutes until soft and pulpy, pressing the berries from time to time to extract the juice.

Strain the fruit and its juices through a jelly bag or some clean muslin suspended over a clean bowl – this will take about 6 hours to allow the fruit left behind to become dry – don't be tempted to squeeze the mixture. Return the strained pulp to a saucepan, add remaining water, bring to the boil and simmer gently for 2 minutes. Strain for another 6 hours, as before.

Measure the juice and pour back into the saucepan. Add 75 g (3 oz) sugar per 100 ml (3½ fl oz) juice. Heat the juice, stirring over a low heat until the sugar is dissolved. Raise the heat and boil rapidly for about 10 minutes until setting point is reached – see page 149. Skim off any surface foam using a flat spoon. Pour into hot jars and seal as described on page 149.

Note: This jelly sets very quickly.

Crab apple jelly

Crab apples are wild apples, often grown as ornamental trees, but the fruit, although too bitter and dry to eat on its own, makes a lovely preserve. Harvest crab apples in September and October, and use as quickly as possible because they don't store well. This recipe also works well with Bramley Apples.

Makes approx. 1 kg (2 lb 3½ oz)

1 kg (2 lb 2 oz) crab apples, well washed
Approx. 1 l (33½ fl oz) water
Approx. 600 g (1 lb 5 oz) granulated sugar

Cut the apples into chunks, removing any bruised bits and put in a large saucepan without peeling or coring and pour over 900 ml (30 fl oz) water. Bring to the boil and simmer gently for 5–10 minutes, stirring and mashing the fruit until soft and pulpy.

Strain the fruit and its juices through a jelly bag or some clean muslin suspended over a clean bowl – this will take about 6 hours to allow the fruit left behind to become dry – don't be tempted to squeeze the mixture. Return the strained pulp to a saucepan and add the remaining water. Bring to the boil, mashing gently, and simmer gently for about 2 minutes. Strain for another 6 hours as before.

Measure the juice and pour back into the saucepan. Add 75 g (3 oz) sugar per 100 ml (3½ fl oz) juice. Heat the juice, stirring over a low heat until the sugar is dissolved. Raise the heat and boil rapidly for 10–15 minutes until setting point is reached – see page 149. Skim off any surface foam using a flat spoon. Pour into hot jars and seal as described on page 149.

Raspberry and rose petal jam

Raspberry jam is delicious but with the added scent of rose petals, the fruitiness is enhanced. Choose unsprayed roses that are just coming into full bloom, and pick them in the morning after the dew has disappeared, before the full sun.

Makes approx. 1.3 kg (3 lb)

2 large heads very fragrant dark red roses
900 g (2 lb) raspberries
900 g (2 lb) granulated sugar
2 tbsp lemon juice
1 tbsp rose water

Separate the petals from the roses. Rinse the petals carefully and gently pat them dry with absorbent kitchen paper. Tear out the white 'heel' from the petals, then tear into thin shreds. Put into a non-metallic bowl and gently stir in the raspberries. Leave in a cool place overnight to allow the flavours to develop.

The next day put the fruit and petals in a large saucepan and mash it with a wooden spoon. Heat gently until steaming. Add the sugar and lemon juice and stir over a low heat until the sugar dissolves. Raise the heat and boil rapidly for 10–15 minutes until setting point is reached – see page 149. Skim off any surface foam using a flat spoon. Stand for 10 minutes then stir to distribute the petals. Add rose water and spoon into hot jars and seal as described on page 149.

Note: Follow the quantities and method above using loganberries and mulberries.

Damson cheese

This is one of the more unusual preserves to serve with hot or cold roast meats. Once it's set, it's so thick you have to slice it, and the flavour is sweet and intense.

Makes approx. 900 g (2lb)

1.35 kg (3 lb) damsons, washed
150 ml (5 fl oz) water
675 g (1½ lb) granulated sugar

Place the damsons in a large saucepan and pour over the water. Bring to the boil, cover and simmer for about 15 minutes until soft and pulpy. Using a slotted spoon, remove as many of the stones as possible, then press the flesh through a nylon sieve. Try to make as much purée as possible – this does take time but you will achieve a greater yield.

Transfer the purée to a saucepan and add the sugar. Heat gently stirring until the sugar has dissolved. Bring to the boil, then reduce to a gentle simmer, and cook for about an hour, stirring occasionally, until the mixture is thick enough to form a trail with a wooden spoon – take care that the mixture doesn't burn on the bottom of the saucepan.

Pour the mixture into 6 x 100 ml (3½ fl oz) sterilised glass jars or moulds – see page 149. Cover with a waxed disc and set aside to cool, then cover as for jam – see page 149. Store in a cool place for about 2 months to mature before serving.

Smoky red tomato jam

Once a jar of this gets opened in my house, it doesn't last long. It goes with so many things: strong flavoured cheeses, freshly cooked bacon, and even smoked fish. Use ripe but firm tomatoes.

Makes approx. 900 g (2 lb)

450 g (1 lb) ripe tomatoes, peeled – see below – and roughly chopped
225 g (8 oz) red onions, peeled and roughly chopped
2 large garlic cloves, peeled and chopped
350 g (12 oz) cooking apples, cored, peeled and roughly chopped
225 ml (8 fl oz) distilled (clear) malt vinegar
175 g (6 oz) granulated sugar
2 tsp smoked sweet paprika
½ tsp cayenne pepper
1½ tsp salt

Put the tomatoes, onion, garlic and apples in a blender or food processor and blend for a few seconds until pulpy and quite smooth. Transfer to a large saucepan and pour over the vinegar. Bring to the boil and simmer gently for 10 minutes, stirring occasionally, until softened. Add the sugar and stir over a low heat until dissolved. Bring to the boil and then simmer steadily for about 15 minutes, stirring occasionally, until the consistency of thick jam. Add paprika, cayenne and salt. Spoon into hot sterilised jars and seal with non-corrosive lids as described on page 149. Allow to cool and store for 6–8 months. Once opened, keep in the fridge and use within 2 weeks.

To peel tomatoes: place in a heatproof bowl and pierce with a fork at the stalk end. Pour over sufficient boiling water to cover and stand for 1–2 minutes until the skins splits. Drain and holding with a fork carefully peel away the skin.

Curried apple chutney

I have a Lord Derby cooking apple tree in my garden, and having just had a bumper crop, you have to get quite inventive with the fruit. Here is a delicious preserve that's the perfect accompaniment to leftover cold Christmas meats!

Makes approx. 1.8 kg (4 lb)

450 g (1 lb) peeled onions, finely chopped
300 ml (10 fl oz) distilled (clear) malt vinegar
900 g (2 lb) cored and peeled cooking apples, finely chopped
2 tsp Madras curry paste
350 g (12 oz) demerara or light brown sugar
115 g (4 oz) no-need-to-soak dried apricots, finely chopped
Salt and freshly ground black pepper

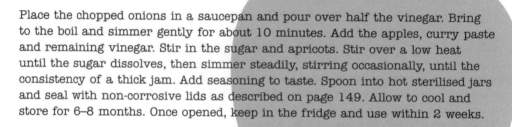

Place the chopped onions in a saucepan and pour over half the vinegar. Bring to the boil and simmer gently for about 10 minutes. Add the apples, curry paste and remaining vinegar. Stir in the sugar and apricots. Stir over a low heat until the sugar dissolves, then simmer steadily, stirring occasionally, until the consistency of a thick jam. Add seasoning to taste. Spoon into hot sterilised jars and seal with non-corrosive lids as described on page 149. Allow to cool and store for 6–8 months. Once opened, keep in the fridge and use within 2 weeks.

Elderflower cordial

If you have an elder tree or one growing near by, it is easy to make your own cordial. Pick the flower heads just as they break into bloom, carefully rinse in cold running water and shake off excess. Trim away as much of the stalk as possible, leaving only the flower heads bunched together.

Makes approx. 600 ml (20 fl oz) undiluted cordial

115 g (4 oz) elderflower heads, washed and trimmed (see above)
500 ml (17 fl oz) water.
350 g (12 oz) caster sugar

Pack the elderflowers into a saucepan and pour over the water. Bring to the boil and simmer gently for 30 minutes.

Strain through muslin and return liquid to the saucepan. Stir in the caster sugar until dissolved, then bring to the boil and simmer for 15 minutes until syrupy and lightly golden. Pour hot into sterilized bottles, seal and cool. Store in the refrigerator for up to 3 months. Serve diluted with water to taste.

Rosehip syrup

A real taste of yester-year. Rosehips are very high in Vitamin C, and because they are in abundance in the hedgerows in late summer, they were widely used in wartime as a vital source of nutrition. Use the hips from wild or dog roses or the cultivated 'Rosa rugosa' – these are the easiest to clean.

Makes approx. 450 ml (15 fl oz)

700 ml (23½ fl oz) water
250 g (9 oz) rosehips, stalks removed and well washed
125 g (4½ oz) granulated sugar

Pour 450 ml (15 fl oz) water into a saucepan and bring to the boil. Mince the rose hips or process in a blender, then place immediately in the boiling water and bring back to the boil. Remove from the heat and allow to stand for 15 minutes.

Strain through a clean jelly bag for about 2 hours to allow the bulk of the juice to drip through. Return the pulp to the saucepan. Bring the remaining water to the boil and pour over the pulp. Stand for a further 10 minutes, then strain as before.

Pour the juice into a clean saucepan, add the sugar and heat gently, stirring, until the sugar dissolves – heat suffiently to dissolve the sugar only, avoid boiling.

Pour the hot syrup into clean sterilized bottles and seal – see page 149. Cool and store in the fridge for up to 3 months. Dilute with water to taste.

Crème anglaise

This is a recipe for 'proper custard' – no custard powder or cornflour in sight. It takes longer to make of course, but it's well worth it!

Makes approx. 650 ml (25 fl oz)

600 ml (20 fl oz) whole milk
1 vanilla pod, split
7 medium free-range egg yolks
75 g (3 oz) caster sugar

Pour the milk into a saucepan and heat until near boiling. Remove from the heat and add the vanilla pod. Set aside to infuse for 30 minutes. Discard the pod.

In a large heatproof bowl, whisk the egg yolks and sugar until pale, thick and creamy, and pour over the vanilla milk, whisking continuously. Stand the bowl over a saucepan of gently simmering water and cook, stirring, until the custard thickens sufficiently to coat the back of the spoon – this will take 20–25 minutes. Pass through a sieve into a serving jug, and serve hot or cold.

Soft fruit coulis

There are several different ways to make this smooth fruit sauce. This is one of the simplest and freshest. It will separate on standing, and is best used within 48 hours of making.

Makes approx. 300 ml (10 fl oz)

115 g (4 oz) strawberries, washed and hulled
115 g (4 oz) raspberries, washed and hulled
115 g (4 oz) blackberries, washed and hulled
4 tbsp unsweetened apple juice
Approx. 1 tbsp locally produced clear honey

Place all the fruit in a blender or food processor and add the apple juice. Blend for a few seconds until smooth. Push through a nylon sieve (strainer) and add sufficient honey to taste. Cover and chill until required.

Note: You can use this method for any of the soft fruits on there own, but you'll need to adjust the sweetening depending on the natural sweetness of the fruit used. Also works well with peaches, plums, and ripe pears.

Sweet pickled dill cucumbers

A great way to enjoy this salad vegetable in another guise after the Summer months have ended. Adds crunch to a ham sandwich, or peps up a Wintry salad no end.

Makes approx. 1 kg (2 lb 3½ oz)

600 g (1 lb 3½ oz) unwaxed large or mini cucumbers
Salt
A few sprigs fresh dill
1 quantity savoury spiced vinegar – see Note below

For large cucumbers, wipe and, without peeling, and cut into 2 cm (¾ in) thick slices. If mini variety, leave whole but pierce all over with a fork. Place a layer of cucumber in a non-reactive bowl and sprinkle generously with salt. Continue filling the bowl ending with a layer of salt. Cover loosely and stand in a cool place for 24 hours.

The next day, rinse well in cold water and then shake off excess water. Pack into a cold one-litre (33½ fl oz) sterilised jar, adding sprigs of dill as you layer. Cover with spiced vinegar and seal with a non-corrosive lid. Allow to mature for 1 month before using. Store in a cool, dark, dry place for up to 6 months – the cucumbers may become soft after this time.

Note: Courgettes and marrow can be pickled using the same method – marrow should be peeled, seeded and diced, whilst courgettes only need slicing, or piercing if baby variety.

For savoury spiced vinegar: mix 1 tbsp each of mustard seeds, black peppercorns and allspice berries with a small piece of root ginger, grated, 1 dried bay leaf and 10 small dried chillies, and then tie in a small square of clean muslin. Add to a saucepan containing 600 ml (20 fl oz) distilled malt vinegar. Bring to the boil and simmer gently for 10 minutes. Stir in 4 tbsp caster sugar. Allow to cool then discard the spice bag. Bottle and store until required. For a less sweet spiced vinegar, reduce or omit the sugar.

Sloe or damson gin

The deep greyish-blue fruit of the hedgerow shrub, blackthorn. Wear gloves to gather sloes in September and October – the thorns are savage. Too bitter to enjoy as a fruit on their own, but using them to flavour gin transforms the liquor into a rich red, warming liqueur that tastes slightly of blackcurrants and almonds. Damson makes a good substitute.

Makes approx. 600 ml (20 fl oz)

350 g (½ oz) sloes or damsons
50 g (2 oz) caster sugar
Approx. 600 ml (20 fl oz), good quality gin

Wash the sloes or damsons thoroughly and pat dry with kitchen paper. Place in a large bowl and prick well with a fork. Transfer to a one-litre (33½ fl oz) sterilised preserving jar and sprinkle in the sugar. Pour over the gin to reach the top. Seal with non-corrosive lids and store in a cool, dark place for at least 2 months – preferably 3 – shaking daily for the first month, until rich red in colour.

Strain into a clean bottle and serve as a liqueur on its own or mix with tonic water for a longer drink.

Bibliography &
Useful Addresses

Elliot, Rose; *Vegetarian Cookery* (Harper Collins, 1992)
Grigson, Jane; *Fruit Book* (Penguin, 1983)
Grigson, Sophie, and William Black; *Fish* (Headline, 1998)
Grigon, Sophie; *Sophie Grigson's Meat Course* (Network Books, 1995)
Larousse Gastronomique (Paul Hamlyn, 1989)
The Cookery Year (Reader's Digest, 1974)

Slow Food A worldwide non-profit-making, eco/gastric, member-supported organisation set up to counteract fast food and fast life. Membership brings with it the opportunity to help your local community, take time to enjoy what's around you and a chance to get involved with like-minded people for the benefit of the environment you live in. www.slowfood.com

FARMA (National Farmers' Retail and Markets Association) Provides independent assessments to standards launched in 2002 to certify farmers' markets in the UK offer the freshest and most local produce. Aims to support the community and local economy, as well as help the environment and reduce air miles. The following websites may be useful:
To find your local market: www.farmersmarkets.net
For farm shops and pick-your-own: www.farma.org.uk
For information on London farmers' markets: www.lfm.org.uk
For information on Scottish farmers' markets: www.scottishfarmersmarkets.co.uk
For information on Welsh farmers' markets: www.fmiw.co.uk

Soil Association Contact www.soilassociation.org for the latest local food issues

www.bigbarn.co.uk UK local food website compiled under England Rural Development programme, supported by DEFRA

Rapeseed oil Cold pressed rapeseed oil is produced in the UK, from one of the few edible oilseeds which grow well in cool and temperate conditions. It has half the saturated fat of olive oil and ten times the Omega 3, and has travelled only a tiny fraction of the food miles olive oil has. Cold pressed rapeseed oil is available all over the UK from specialist retailers. For more information call 01890 885010 or visit www.oleifera.co.uk.

Atholl Glens Organic Beef and Lamb is a farming co-operative on the Atholl Estates in Highland Perthshire, one of the UK's largest special protection areas. Mutton is also available. Mail order delivery service across the UK. Tel: 01796 481 482 or visit www.athollglens.co.uk.

Index

Apple sauce 152
Asparagus envelopes 35

Bacon wrapped monkfish brochettes 58
Baked brill with pea salsa and samphire 24
Baked mushrooms with haggis and sweet and sour sauce 100
Baked sea bass with fragrant herbs and fennel 55
Barbecued lettuce salad 64
Barbecued quail with fragrant spices and sweet pepper relish 52
Beef in red wine with green beans and morel mushrooms 14
Beef Wellington parcels with damson sauce 82
Black pudding and scallop salad 125
Blackberry meringue crush with sweet cider apple sauce 102
Blackcurrant ice cream 73
Blueberry Arctic roll 68
Blueberry jam 159
Bonfire night toffee apples 103
Bramble (blackberry) jelly 158
Broad bean falafels 34
Buttered skate in parchment 127

cakes: Chocolate chestnut cake with coffee icing 140
    Chocolate raspberry squidgy cakes 106
    Extra indulgent cream tea scones and jam 41
    Glazed berry custard tarts 75
    Spiced pear and blackberry cake 108
    Wild strawberry Viennese shortcakes 74
Carrot and ginger pudding 141
Cauliflower and broccoli gratin 98
Celeriac gratin 133
Cheesy crumb stuffed courgettes and marrow 63
Chocolate cherry roulade 71
Chocolate chestnut cake with coffee icing 140
Chocolate raspberry squidgy cakes 106
Christmas roast goose with sage and onion stuffing 119
chutneys: method 148–149
Cinnamon toast and buttered apples 138
Cockle and clam chowder 22
Coronation chicken with fresh peach salsa 51
Crab apple jelly 164
Crab cakes with green mayonnaise 25
Creamed horseradish relish 155
Creamy Jerusalem artichoke and potato bake 135

Crème anglaise 171
Crumble topped plum pie 104
Curried apple chutney 168
Curried parsnip bhajis 137

Damson cheese 166
Deep fried haddock and chips 126
desserts: Blackberry meringue crush with sweet cider apple sauce 102
    Blackcurrant ice cream 73
    Blueberry Arctic roll 68
    Carrot and ginger pudding 141
    Chocolate cherry roulade 71
    Cinnamon toast and buttered apples 138
    Crumble topped plum pie 104
    Easter meringue nests with chocolate-dipped strawberries 40
    Elderflower sorbet 39
    Fragrant slow-baked quince 107
    Fresh peach melba 69
    Gooseberry cheesecake 38
    Greengage and almond ricotta cream trifle 72
    Honeyed hazelnut tart 143
    Mulled wine pear syllabub 105
    My Granny's rhubarb pie 36
    Rhubarb fool crème brulées 37
    Rhubarb and tangerine dumpling 142
    Roast pears with whisky and oat cream 139
    Soft fruit terrine 70
    Squash and treacle tart 109

Easter 'Guard of Honour' with leek and rosemary stuffing 17
Easter meringue nests with chocolate-dipped strawberries 40
Elderflower cordial 169
Elderflower sorbet 39
Extra indulgent cream tea scones and jam 41

Fire-cooked potato and corn skewers 65
fish and shellfish: Bacon wrapped monkfish brochettes 58
    Baked brill with pea salsa and samphire 24
    Baked sea bass with fragrant herbs and fennel 55
    Black pudding and scallop salad 125
    Buttered skate in parchment 127
    Cockle and clam chowder 22
    Crab cakes with green mayonnaise 25
    Deep fried haddock and chips 126
    Fresh tuna with fresh bean salad 59
    Grilled mackerel with sherry vinegar and shallot relish 94

Grilled sardines on toast with fresh tomato salsa 56
Halibut en croute with julienne vegetables 27
Home smoked trout with rosemary 57
John Dory with garlic potatoes 92
Kedgeree 90
Mackerel in oatmeal with rhubarb sauce 23
Moules with creamy garlic liquor 130
Oyster Po'boy sandwich 93
Oyster and scallop stew 89
Pasta with roast salmon and asparagus 21
Plaice and crab roulades en gratin 28
Potted shrimps 60
Roast langoustines with smoky garlic mayo 129
Salad of strawberries, smoked salmon and cucumber 67
Smoked fish cakes with beetroot 91
Soupe de poisson 47
Spanish-style seafood rice 54
Walnut and goat's cheese crusted cod 128
Forestière potatoes 101
Fragrant slow-baked quince 107
freezing 147–148
Fresh cream of tomato and basil soup 12
Fresh peach melba 69
Fresh tomato sauce 157
Fresh tuna with fresh bean salad 59

game: Barbecued quail with fragrant spices and sweet pepper relish 52
    Hot pigeon with pear and red cabbage salad 124
    Roast grouse with bread sauce and parsnip game chips 88
    Roast partridge with plum and Madeira sauce 86
    Venison and juniper pie 122
    Warm guinea fowl salad with lavender dressing 85
    Wild duck with quince mash 87
Gammon and apple cobbler 118
Glazed berry custard tarts 75
Globe artichokes with hot mayonnaise 61
Gooseberry cheesecake 38
Gooseberry curd 161
Greengage and almond ricotta cream trifle 72
Grilled mackerel with sherry vinegar and shallot relish 94
Grilled sardines on toast with fresh tomato salsa 56

Haggis, neeps and tattie pie 120
Halibut en croute with julienne vegetables 27
Ham, chicken and leek picnic pie 49
Ham shank with peas and parsley sauce 18
Herb and garlic oil 151
Herby egg rolls of chicken, cucumber and pea shoots 19
Home smoked trout with rosemary 57
Homemade stock 156
Honey glazed sausages with mustard and onion mash 84
Honeyed hazelnut tart 143
Hot pigeon with pear and red cabbage salad 124

jam: method 148–149
John Dory with garlic potatoes 92

Kedgeree 90

Lavender vinegar 150
Leek and wild garlic soup 13
Liver and onions with colcannon mash 121

Mackerel in oatmeal with rhubarb sauce 23
Mayonnaise 154
Mediterranean sweet pepper and squash soup 80
Mint sauce 152
Mixed bean and bacon picnic loaf 62
Moroccan spiced lamb shanks with crushed pumpkin 83
Moroccan-style spinach and chicken pie 15
Moules with creamy garlic liquor 130
Moussaka 48
Mulled wine pear syllabub 105
Mushroom and buckwheat crepe bake 96
Mustardy vegetable croustades 131
Mutton and barley broth 115
Mutton, potato and spinach curry 117
My Granny's rhubarb pie 36

Oyster Po'boy sandwich 93
Oyster and scallop stew 89

Pasta with roast salmon and asparagus 21

Pasta with spinach, blue cheese, pine nuts and raisins 31
Pea tarts 33
Peach conserve 160
Perfect gravy 154
Perfect roast roots 134
Piri piri pork with chilli dressing 53
Plaice and crab roulades en gratin 28
Potted shrimps 60
poultry: Christmas roast goose with sage and onion stuffing 119
   Coronation chicken with fresh peach salsa 51
   Ham, chicken and leek picnic pie 49
   Herby egg rolls of chicken, cucumber and pea shoots 19
   Moroccan-style spinach and chicken pie 15
   Three bird roast 123
Pressed tomato moulds with goat's cheese 29
Pumpkin butter 162

Raspberry and rose petal jam 155
Ratatouille-stuffed pork 50
Redcurrant jelly 153
Rhubarb fool crème brulées 37
Rhubarb and tangerine dumpling 142
Roast grouse with bread sauce and parsnip game chips 88
Roast langoustines with smoky garlic mayo 129
Roast partridge with plum and Madeira sauce 86
Roast pears with whisky and oat cream 139
Root vegetable pottage 114
Rosehip syrup 170
Rowan and apple jelly 163

salads: Barbecued lettuce salad 64
   Black pudding and scallop salad 125
   Salad of strawberries, smoked salmon and cucumber 67
   Warm guinea fowl salad with lavender dressing 85
Sloe or damson gin 173

Slow roast onions with goat's cheese 99
Slow roast pork belly with apple mash 20
Smoked fish cakes with beetroot 91

Smoky red tomato jam 167
Smoky sweet corn chowder 46
Soft fruit coulis 171
Soft fruit terrine 70
Soupe de poisson 47
soups: Cockle and clam chowder 22
   Fresh cream of tomato and basil soup 12
   Leek and wild garlic soup 13
   Mediterranean sweet pepper and squash soup 80
   Mutton and barley broth 115
   Root vegetable pottage 114
   Smoky sweet corn chowder 46
   Soupe de poisson 47
   Wild mushroom soup 81
Spanish-style oxtail stew with chilli dough boys 116
Spanish-style seafood rice 54
Spiced pear and blackberry cake 108
Spiced red cabbage with blackberries and apple 97
Spring lamb noisettes with mint and caramelised salsify 16
Spring vegetable frittata 32
Squash and blue cheese risotto 95
Squash and treacle tart 109
Stir fried spring cabbage 30
Stir-fried Winter greens with bacon and chestnuts 132
Sweet onion and cheesy bread 136
Sweet pickle dill cucumbers 172

Thick sole goujons with cucumber tartare sauce 26
Three bird roast 123
Tian of Provençale vegetables 66

Venison and juniper pie 122

Walnut and goat's cheese crusted cod 128
Warm guinea fowl salad with lavender dressing 85
Wild duck with quince mash 87
Wild mushroom soup 81
Wild strawberry Viennese shortcakes 74

Acknowledgements

Special thanks to my Mum and to Tilly Wilton, for their help with recipe testing; to Craig Copland of the Handy Shop in Crieff for helping me compile the seasonal fruit and vegetable guides, and for sourcing produce for my recipe testing; to Murray Lauchlan of David Comrie and Son butcher's in Comrie for sourcing the game meats, and to John Dakers of Atholl Glens for help sourcing mutton. As ever, thank you to all my family and fiends for their tireless and invaluable tasting skills.